To: Lester,

Keep leading and succeeding!

Blessings

My

Brother's

Keeper

ALSO BY DR. EDDIE M. CONNOR, JR.

Purposefully Prepared to Persevere

Collections of Reflections, Volumes 1-3:
Symphonies of Strength

E.CON the ICON: from Pop Culture to
President Barack Obama

Unwrap The Gift In You

Heal Your Heart

My Brother's Keeper

Rebuilding, Reconciling, and Restoring The Lives of Boys and Men

Dr. Eddie M. Connor, Jr.

My Brother's Keeper and other books by Dr. Eddie M. Connor, Jr. may be purchased in bulk for educational, business, or sales promotional use. For information, please e-mail the Administrative and Markets Department at info@EddieConnor.com.

FIRST EDITION

All scripture references are from the King James Version, New King James Version, and New International Version Bible.

Library of Congress Cataloging-in-Publication Data has been applied for.

ISBN: 978-0-9970504-0-0

10 9 8 7 6 5 4 3 2 1

This book is dedicated to the boys and young men, that I have taught and mentored through the years. I celebrate the next generation leaders in middle schools, high schools, and college campuses across America. You are the leaders of tomorrow, that you have been looking for today. Greatness flows through your DNA. More than ever, unwrap your gifts and unlock your limitless potential within. You can see farther, because you stand on the shoulders of giants, who have come before you.

Thank you for allowing me, to place deposits of determination and value in your life. You may not realize it, but you taught me too. I can say that I am a better man today, because of the life lessons I learned from you.

CONTENTS

My

Brother's

Keeper

FOR MORE ON
MY BROTHER'S KEEPER

VISIT:
WWW.EDDIECONNOR.COM

INTRODUCTION

Against All Odds

I remember like it was yesterday. I was a senior in high school, sitting in my guidance counselor's office. Much like many of the seniors in my class, I was called to the office over the PA system. We were all awaiting the news regarding college acceptance letters, updates, and opportunities for the future. So, on one hand I was excited, but on the other hand I was shaking in my Air Jordan shoes. I was hoping this would be a slam dunk.

Sitting in that office, while my guidance counselor perused my grades, all I could hear was the clock on the wall ticking. The silence was deafening. The rapper Eminem, had not released the verse to the song, *Lose Yourself* at this time, but my "palms were sweaty,

1

knees weak, and arms were heavy." I was on tiptoe anticipation. All I could think about, was breaking the news to my family and friends, about what my guidance counselor, was soon to tell me. I couldn't wait to hear the news about college and opportunities, to change my life.

Here it was, the moment of truth. My eyes were fastened to her, as she slowly turned around in her squeaky office chair. My counselor took a deep breath, looked at my grades, and pursed her lips.

She said, "Well, Eddie I don't know." I thought to myself, "You don't know, what time it is? You don't know, what time I go to lunch? What don't you know?" All of a sudden, she began to say, "Eddie I don't think you're college material. You have not been accepted to any colleges. I don't see higher education being an option for you, much less community college."

She went on to tell me, that I should consider

picking up a trade, in some sort of skilled job area. I realize that my ACT score and grade point average, was her only barometer to measure who I was, and what I could become. People will often judge you, based on where you are, not where they think you can go.

As I think in retrospect, the individual was the furthest thing from a "guidance counselor." None of her words were positive, affirming, guidance driven, or substantive for my future. Sitting in that office, the impending anticipation of joy and jubilation, turned to sadness and sorrow. Have you ever cried on the inside and held back the tears, so it wouldn't show on the outside?

At that moment, it was like a dart struck through my heart. She immediately yelled, "Next" for another senior to come in and take a seat. This was an "academic assembly line" that crushed my dreams.

How many young people today, were just like me?

Our children hear disconcerting words in minutes, that alter their lives for years, simply because of their present situation.

As a 17-year-old senior, walking out of her office, all I could think of was my future and how bleak it looked. Here I was, standing in the shadows of my struggles, because my life was dealt with yet another blow. I was so disappointed, that I became numb to the internal pain. All I could think was "Why me? Why now? Here we go again."

Just a few years ago, at the age of 15, I received bad news from a doctor who diagnosed me with *NHL*. I can only say comically today, that *NHL,* for me then meant *National Hockey League*. I wish the news conveyed, that I was going to be the owner of a *National Hockey League* franchise. Wishful thinking! Yet the real life reality, was that I was diagnosed with stage four cancer. The diagnosis of *NHL*, stood for *Non-Hodgkin's Lymphoma*. The health diagnosis I received, was practically a death sentence.

In spite of the specter of death, I had to speak life into my life. I proclaimed, "I shall not die, but live and declare the works of the Lord" (Psalm 118:17). The power of death and life comes out of your mouth, because your words create your world. I've learned that what you profess, is ultimately what you will possess.

Life will process what you profess, framing the scope of what you will ultimately possess. Make a habit of thinking and speaking positive, even when negativity is staring you in the face.

According to the American Childhood Cancer Organization, "Roughly 1 in 285 children in the U.S. will be diagnosed with cancer before their 20th birthday." What were the odds, of me being that one? The words, "Why me?" rang so loudly in my mind. I endured chemotherapy and radiation, five days a week for 18 months. Not only losing my hair, but my self-confidence, self-esteem, and self-motivation to live.

Seemingly every odd and individual was against me, including my father who never supported me in my struggle. Where was my keeper, when I went through cancer, as my father was absent in my life? Where were the people who dropped me, when they should have helped me? These questions that reside in my mind, I may never know the answers to. Without God and my praying mother, Dr. Janice Connor, you would never read these words from me today. Who I am and what I have become, is a byproduct of how I have grappled and endured the trials of life.

Sadly, the guidance counselor, never provided an ounce of guidance. Regardless as to how they discouraged me, I encouraged myself to persevere in spite of negative news. I decided to not go negative on the negative, but to think positive in a negative situation.

I pushed myself to attend college, in spite of what people thought about me. I went on to attend and graduate from college three times, earning a Ph.D., which for that guidance counselor it stood for a "player hater degree."

Yes, cancer made me cry, but it didn't make me quit. I discovered, the first three letters in "cancer" is "CAN." You CAN overcome. You CAN persevere. You CAN prove the doubters, haters, naysayers, and cynics wrong. You "CAN do all things through Christ, that strengthens you" (Philippians 4:13). Against all the odds, that are stacked against you, don't give up. You CAN make it! You're alive because you've survived. Now it's time to thrive!

This is the messaging, that our boys and young men must hear. Stories of struggle, transformed into strength. We have to lift up our voice and speak louder, than the music blaring through their headphones. We have to love our brothers, despite the mistakes they make. We must coach them through life, present opportunities to execute, and cheer them on to victory, like fans at a sports game.

This is why I have dedicated my life, to mentoring and uplifting our youth. I am particularly dedicated, to empower our boys and young men. I am engaged in the work to develop their literacy and life skills via my mentoring program, *Boys 2 Books*.

When I began to realize that I am *My Brother's Keeper*, it moved me from selfishness to selflessness. From seeking to compete, to looking for opportunities to collaborate and sow seeds into the next generation.

We have a society of lost men, who are searching to find themselves in a false sense of bravado. Manhood is more than being macho with money, muscles, a mansion, Mercedes, and a phone full of numbers from ladies.

Real manhood is about your mentality above the

neck, not what you possess below the waist. Manhood is about respect and responsibility, that governs personal life laws for how you represent yourself daily in the community. Only real men, can remedy real issues.

As the author, of *My Brother's Keeper*, I wrote this book unfiltered, unscripted, and unapologetic. It details the plight, promise, and systemic ills that are socially engineered, to impede the progress of our Black brothers.

My aim is not to leave you, in a paralyzing predicament of peril, but to provide pragmatic solutions. I believe that you will find the solutions to be advantageous. The adapted methods and measures, will strengthen you, your school, family, and community. Business as usual can no longer be tolerable. When we are united, we are formidable to overcome every obstacle.

Use this book as a manual, to manage your purpose, and manifest your destiny. As you read this book, I challenge you to find a partner, that will hold you accountable to your goals, educational achievements, spiritual commitment, personal development, and lifelong progression. This individual may be a mentor, teacher, father, pastor, peer, or fellow friend. As they are an advocate for you, become a greater advocate for yourself and others. The life lessons that you learn from them, can be used to empower someone else to where you can truly say, "I am *My Brother's Keeper*."

Reach out and share your story. I want to hear from you, as to how this book has empowered you or someone that you know, in the classroom or community. Proceeds from the sale of this book, will go to support the literacy/ mentoring program, *Boys 2 Books*.

I often say, "The revolution will not be televised, it will be digitized." So, log on and connect with me, at www.EddieConnor.com, join me there for more information and inspiration.

As you know, social media is the norm of our digital age. I want you to be educationally, mentally, and spiritually F.I.T., so connect with me on Facebook, Instagram, and Twitter: **@EddieConnorJr** (social media handle). Be sure to use the hashtag, **#MyBrothersKeeper** and/or **#MBK**. I'm looking forward to inspiring you, on this literary journey!

I AM…MY BROTHER'S KEEPER!

CHAPTER 1

Saving Our Sons

T he persistent and resounding question in America, is "How do we save our boys, our sons, and our brothers?" Generally when this question is posed, it's directly aimed at the plight of Black and Hispanic males. At its core, I believe that we're searching, for the remedy to heal broken men.

The great leader of the abolitionist movement, Frederick Douglass declared, "It is easier to build strong children, than to repair broken men." I'd like to put a new millennium remix on it and say, "If we build strong boys, we won't have to repair broken men." Simply because our society would have you to believe, that there is more plight and peril, than promise for Black and Hispanic males.

FROM SAVING TO BUILDING

When will we shift our focus, from saving to building? The power of building, places the onus of responsibility on each of us, to equip our brothers with the skills to innovate and provide stability in their community. None of us has the power to save all of us. However, each of us, has the innate ability to work together, to build all of us.

We holler "Save our Black males" like we're waiting on some outside entity, to do what we can do ourselves. Our brothers are not charity cases. Society would rather them be pitied, than empowered. The bricks of our struggle and strength, can be used to provide a foundation for our brothers to build their lives.

SOS

The SOS, to "Save Our Sons" is more than a slogan. Above all, it's a call to action. If we turn our back on our brothers, we leave them at the behest of systemic racism and societal forces. In essence, our brothers have become "the stones that the builders rejected" (Psalm 118:22).

When you begin to see yourself as a builder, you will harness your greatness. As a builder, you will begin to use every stumbling block, as a stepping stone. Open your eyes of faith and begin to see yourself, as a visionary builder. We must awaken to the fact, that each of us are under construction. As a result, we must be transparent in strengthening and sharpening one another.

IRON MAN

Proverbs 27:17 declares, "Iron sharpeneth iron; so a man sharpeneth the countenance of his friend." A real *Iron Man,* a real friend, and brother will instruct you, in order to sharpen you for the journey ahead. It's time to roll up your sleeves, put on your hard hat, and forge ahead to build up your brothers. To do that, we must do more than be judgmentally dismissive. Rather we must "pardon their dust" because at the end of the day, we are all under construction.

None of us are perfect and has it all together. When you fail to analyze your flaws, by perpetuating a false sense of bravado then pride will be the downfall of your ego. Real men keep it real with their brothers and continue to fight, turning struggles into strengths. This must be an "all hands on deck" approach, to building our brothers and uplifting our communities.

IF IT AIN'T BROKE, DON'T FIX IT

When will we shake off this "do nothing" approach? I'm

tired of hearing people say, "It's not my problem" or "Somebody else will do it." The "it will fix itself" concept never works. People are notorious for saying, "If it ain't broke, don't fix it." Well, start looking around you. The system is beyond broken.

Our communities, schools, and homes are fractured and shattered. It's beyond being reformed, it must be transformed. It's about time we do something to fix it! It's going to take all of us, pushing our egos aside, in efforts to strengthen, sharpen, and stabilize our communities. It begins from within and starts with us. We are the repairers of the breach and the restorers of the streets!

"ILLUSION OF INCLUSION"

The obtrusive and overt roots of racism, have become an obnoxious alarm clock, awakening America out of it's cultural coma. The ascension of President Barack Obama, being the first Black man to occupy the White House, brought about celebrations extolling race relations.

Many ingested a societal sedative, only to believe that racism in America was officially dead. In fact racism has never received an inscribed tombstone or had risen from the dead, because it has always been alive. On the verge of an American race war, we have seen the unending assault on Black bodies at the hands of police. These tragedies have in fact awakened a sleeping giant, that being the conscience of Black America.

It's quite unnerving to suggest, that we live in a post-racial society. In fact we are living, in a most racial society. We continue to see Black boys and men, killed at the hands of White police officers, sworn to protect and serve.

Black faces in high places, does not mean that everything is "all good." In fact, it generally means the opposite. Slavery has taken on a new form, with the advent of the prison industrial complex. Voting rights are being repealed and amended with voter ID laws. Racism is bipolar, because it continues to transition from covert to overt and vice versa.

There is a new Jim Crow of illiteracy, being interconnected to incarceration. In America's past, lynchings occurred, once every four days. Presently, Black males are victims of police brutality, every two or three days. We continue to see, modern day lynchings of our brothers.

Consequently, our brothers are instantaneously relegated to becoming social media hashtags, rather than heralded as social movement heroes. Tragically, we have become familiar with the names of Oscar Grant, Trayvon Martin, Michael Brown, Tamir Rice, Freddie Gray, Eric Garner, Walter Scott, Laquan McDonald, and a host of other victims of vitriolic racial violence.

So, it begs the question, "What is the value of Black life in America?" More money is invested into the prison system, than the education system. It is evident, that incarceration is the focus, rather than education. A disproportionate rate of Black and Hispanic males, are apart of incarceration nation.

We are witnessing an "Illusion of Inclusion" (coined by Patricia Pope). Strides for cultural assimilation, does not negate the annihilation of Black communities and Black bodies. Our boys are facing exclusion in society and expulsion in schools, more than ever before.

Have we made any substantive progress, since the Selma-to-Montgomery March of 1965? We crossed the Edmund Pettis Bridge, but have we symbolically been pushed back, only to find our people surrounded by rage and racism? The "Bloody Sunday" historical inference has now transpired, in a digital age, Monday through Saturday. Surely, there are more bridges that we must cross and barriers to overcome.

PRISON PIPELINE

Illiteracy is a major factor, which has given rise to the school-to-prison pipeline. According to the American School Board Journal, "What happens in schools (or fails to happen) determines, in large part, whether young people enter the criminal justice system." There has been no advent of legislative or substantive "Drano" to unclog, this impending preschool-to-prison pipeline.

According to the Civil Rights Data Collection (CRDC), "Black children represent only 18 percent of preschool enrollment nationally, but make up 42 percent of students suspended once and nearly half of students, who are suspended more than once."

The inequality in society and the school system, has

markedly created a path for our brothers to be locked in prison, rather than unlock their dreams at Princeton.

As educators, teachers, and mentors we are now placed in a precarious position to help our brothers live, survive, and thrive in a society, that has forecasted their failure.

LEADERSHIP VOID OF LOVE

Dr. Cornel West poignantly suggests, "You can't save the people, if you won't serve the people. You can't lead them, if you don't love them." Who do you turn to, when the people that should nurture and love you, now turn on you or away from you? Sadly, these are the sentiments from many of our boys and men.

There are too many leaders, void of love. They have the title as a leader, but lack the essence of a leader. They have the leadership position, but lack the love and discipline, to function in the position.

As a result, our brothers have become societal outcasts, throwaways, overlooked, underserved, and underrepresented. They are unloved, not only by the larger society, but oftentimes in their own community. We see too many forces, preying on the lives of our brothers, rather than people praying for the lives of our brothers.

We have heard so much deficit language, about Black and Hispanic males in America. Sadly, our brothers have begun to identify with what they see and hear about themselves the most. We must use words that create possibilities, rather than assassinate opportunities.

ABCD

We have to switch the negative to the positive, with Asset-Based building language. Our brothers are not pariahs and predators, we are protectors. We are not liabilities, we are assets to our communities, schools, and universities. We are not pimps, players, and drug pushers, we are doctors, lawyers, astrophysicists, entrepreneurs, community innovators, engineers, and architects who build the future. We are game changers, radical revolutionaries, movers and shakers, who stand on the shoulders of giants. We always talk about, what is missing and broken in our community, that we fail to recognize who is making a difference in our community.

My brother you are NOT a statistic. You are a standout. You are NOT a liability. You are an asset to you community and university. You are a resource and the story of your resilience, will resurrect hope in someone's life. The positive stories that we share about ourselves, has to be greater than the negative depiction painted about our image. We are the sum of what we say about ourselves. This is the asset-based language that must become the norm in our barbershops, schools, recreation centers, places of worship, and communities.

The power of Asset-Based language, leads to Asset-Based Community Development (ABCD). This approach is a way of working with communities, to focus on collective strengths and assets. ABCD focuses on seeing the glass half-full, rather than half-empty. It pushes us to be optimistic, rather than pessimistic in order to remedy realistic issues. This approach represents the ideal that despite impending struggles, communities have many strengths, from which to build upon. ABCD is built on four foundations, (Kretzmann, 2010; Kretzmann & McKnight, 1993; Mathie & Cunningham, 2003):

1. It focuses on community assets and strengths, rather than problems and needs.

2. It identifies and mobilizes individual and community assets, skills, and passions.

3. It is community driven, building communities from the inside out.

4. It is relationship driven, fostering connections with each other.

The foundation of our communities, has been built upon a liability ABCD approach of Animosity, Blight, Carnage, and Degradation. Our communities have been socially engineered to harbor self-hate, violence, abuse, addiction, and transform dreams into nightmares. When we recognize that we are a people, who are greater than negativity and begin to imbibe self-love, we will translate that to our brothers and sisters in our communities.

The basic building blocks, of a liability-free ABCD approach are focused on the strengths, despite the glaring weaknesses that may be evident. When we begin to see that youth can achieve, despite their frailties, we can then provide information and instruction that uplifts them.

AT-RISK

The asset-based approach changes the perspective to

acknowledge our youth as assets, rather than liabilities. It eliminates deficit conversation, that focuses on our brothers and youth as being "at-risk." How many times do you hear, that our youth are "at-risk?" All the negative adjectives and statistics, are placed concurrently with that phrase. Surprisingly you rarely, if ever, hear that our youth are "at-promise." If we fashion and build our youth the right way, they will build upon the promise of achieving their goals. Our youth will build upon the promise, of overcoming obstacles and seeing their value.

The forces that seek to perpetuate inequality, has left our people in a precarious position of being at-risk to the streets and prisons, due to inequality in education and lack of access to opportunities.

Nothing worth working for comes easy. The true test of one's faith is what you're willing to risk, for the enhancement of a person's life. We must take the risk to build the lives of those who are deemed "at-risk."

If we build and train up our children, in the way that they should go, they will bring their vision to fruition. When they're older, they won't depart from the training. When our brothers are older, they won't go to prison they will going to Princeton. When they're older, they won't go to jail, they will going to Cornel and Yale. When they're older, our brothers won't serve four years in a prison house. They will do four years at Morehouse. When they're older they won't go to a correctional facility, they will go to a college or university.

Essentially they will flip the negative, positively. Our people will truly be "at-risk" of realizing their dream, "at-risk" of going to college, "at-risk" of uplifting their communities, "at-risk" of starting a business, and "at-risk" of being their brother's and sister's keeper. The indictment is that we continually see, what we continue to speak. We

27

continue to portray, what we perpetuate. Ironically, our words continue to create the world, in which we reside.

SERVANT LEADER

The essence of leadership hinges, on what you're willing to let go of to gain. You can't lead, if you don't love. You can't build and save, if you won't bless and serve. So many times we see life, as an ESPN highlight reel and become blinded by the lights. Leadership is not what takes place in the lights, the fundamental form of it is forged through character in the dark. People will open their eyes to admire the fruits of your labor, but close a blind eye to the seeds you sowed to reap the harvest.

We are the supermen that we have been looking for, time and time again. We are the servant leaders, who can forge something great in our communities. The essence of servant leadership, goes beyond a title and seeks to commit its time. Servant leadership is more concerned about reconciliation, than recognition. This type of leadership, is ingrained in devotion to a worthy cause.

Dr. King declared, "Everybody can be great, because anybody can serve. You don't have to have a college degree to serve. You don't have to make your subject and verb agree to serve. You only need a heart full of grace. A soul generated by love." A heart of grace, a soul of love, and a mind to serve, is what will transform males into men of destiny, who manifest their purpose in the community. Simply because, the greatest leader is a servant leader.

The concept of "servant leadership" was coined by Robert K. Greenleaf. In his essay, *The Servant As Leader* he wrote, "The servant-leader is servant first. It begins with the natural feeling that one wants to serve. Then conscious choice brings one to aspire to lead." Greenleaf goes on to suggest, "The servant makes sure that other people's highest priority needs are being served. The best test, and difficult to administer, is: Do those served grow as persons? Do they, become healthier, wiser, freer, more autonomous, more likely themselves to become servants? And, what is the effect on the least privileged in society? Will they benefit or at least not be further deprived?"

The power of serving and leading has to be a calling. Formal education, accolades, success, money, and having more degrees than a thermometer, is not the litmus test of leadership. The substantive framework is via the foundation of servitude. The life and ministry of Jesus, provides the greatest example of servant leadership. In Matthew 23:11, Jesus declared, "He that is greatest among you shall be your servant."

STRUCTURE AND FUNCTION

The structure of servant leadership, is about making the

goals clear and then rolling up your sleeves, to help others succeed. In that vein, they don't work for you, but you work for them. Leadership is more than a title or a position, it's a function. Since it is a function, you must take action.

Real leadership causes you to be self-reflective. The question is: Are you here to do something, or are you here just for something to do? If you're on this planet to do something, then what is it? What difference will you make? What will be your legacy? What's your passion? What's your drive? What is it that energizes you? Other than your alarm clock, what wakes you up in the morning? How excellent do you want to be? Do you want to be good or great, average or amazing, ordinary or extraordinary?

Possessing passion is not enough, you must transform your passion into action. What you dedicate yourself to, has to consume you each day. You must find the motivation and inspiration within. It must be authentic. You can't be lackadaisical and lazy. Nothing worth working for is easy, that's why it's called hard work.

Life is not social media, it's not about how many people like you. It's really about how much love, you have for yourself and others. You can't reflect love, if you don't possess love within. Real leadership isn't measured by the number of followers, that someone has on Facebook, Instagram, Periscope, and Twitter. Real leadership is about the number of leaders, that one creates. True leadership must be for the benefit of the followers, not to just enrich the leader.

POPULARITY OR PERFORMANCE

Leadership is not about popularity, it's about performance. When you're committed to the task at hand, you will be committed to be the best that you can be. When you realize that you have untapped potential and power, you will know that what is on the outside, is never greater than what is on the inside.

RELATIONAL LEADERSHIP

Leaders are not dictatorial, they are relational. They build caring and committed relationships with others that go beyond *I* and *Me*, to focus on *Us* and *We*. Real leaders operate from a "show and tell" standpoint, because they lead by example to where their actions do the talking. Too many people's lips are moving, but their actions aren't saying anything.

There is no true leadership, without ownership and sometimes that means saying, "I messed up." Just because you messed up, doesn't mean you have to give up. A knockdown is not a knockout, unless you stay down. Get back up and get back in the fight. Brush your shoulders off and learn from your mistakes.

MISTAKES AND MENTORS

During my time, as a student at Eastern Michigan University, I worked as a Resident Advisor and became a campus leader. I can remember, there was a pertinent and poignant quote that was placed on our staff shirts, which read, "Life teaches you in two ways: Mistakes and Mentors." Leaders have mentors, because they're always learning and aren't afraid of accountability. If they make a mistake they identify it, learn from it, and rectify it. How can you heal it, if you refuse to deal with it?

William Arthur Ward declared, "We must be silent before we can listen. We must listen before we can learn. We must learn before we can prepare. We must prepare before we can serve. We must serve before we can lead." True success comes as a result of service and sacrifice. Leaders are not only judged by how well they lead, but they are judged by how well they serve.

Leadership is not what it says, leadership is what it does. There are no BIG *I's* and little *U's*, when it comes to being a leader. A true leader is more concerned about *WE,* instead of *ME*! They understand without *WE*, there is no *ME.*

WHICH ONE ARE YOU?

Your experiences don't disqualify you. In fact, they have qualified you to lead. You have to see yourself as the best, act like you're the best, and work together to be the best. Leaders are not whiners, they're winners. Leaders are not chumps, they're champions. Leaders are not worriers, they're warriors. Leaders are not chickens, they're eagles. Which one are you? It's time to soar and lift your brother to the next level, but you can't elevate by thinking small. Stretch your mind to think BIG!

Real leaders have more than just sight, they have vision. Having sight without vision, just means you're still

35

blind. Anybody can see a problem, but it takes vision to find a solution. Leadership is more about what you DO, than what you SAY.

FROM IMPOSSIBLE, TO I'M POSSIBLE

Nelson Mandela said, "It always looks impossible, until it's done." How could he say that? Simply because, Mandela was the nation's conscience and a moral leader of the world. He was a man of peace, in a time of war. In an age of apathy, Mandela took action. As a political activist, he opposed a government that inflicted violence, on its people. In 1962, Mandela was ultimately imprisoned for 27 years, because he challenged the archaic ideologies of injustice.

He was incarcerated, isolated on Robben Island, and had insurmountable odds stacked against him. Yet, he didn't let it rob him of his commitment to his people. He used the pain, to make him powerful. In 1994, Mandela used the negative as a building block, to become the first Black president of South Africa at 75 years of age. It's not too late to be great, neither is it too early to get started. Just like Mandela stood up to apartheid and injustice, you too can provide hope and opportunity in your community. Begin to lead with love, push forward with faith, and overcome every obstacle. Adjust your vision, to see every *Impossible* as *I'm Possible*. Find the *CAN* in every *Can't* and grow through every situation.

To live out your purpose and maximize your potential, takes courage to shine even in dark times. Anybody can be a leader when things are going well, but where do you stand when challenges come? Dr. King expressed, "The ultimate measure of a man, is not where he stands in moments of comfort and convenience, but where he stands at times of challenge and controversy."

WHAT'S ON THE MENU?

Just because a few people have aspired to greatness, in the Black community via politics, business, entertainment, or athletics, does not mean that all have now been granted a seat at the table. Someone told me, "If you're not at the table, then you're on the menu."

Time and time again, our brothers are eaten alive by societal forces, that seek to relegate them to a cycle of negativity. No outside force will save our sons. We will only win, from within. We have to come together to break the cycle and create opportunities, so our young men won't drown in a cesspool of calamity. It is incumbent upon us, who have risen out of the ashes of apathy and acrimony, to invest into the lives of those who are seeking to do the same. We have to give of our time, talent, and treasure by sowing seeds of strength into the communities we come from.

DO SOMETHING WITH IT

In his book, *The Souls of Black Folk,* sociologist and Pan-Africanist, W.E.B. Du Bois lays claim to the fact, that those who are the "Talented Tenth" have to invest into the ninety of our greater society. What will we do, with all of our talent, oftentimes lying dormant. We must affect change for others, that goes beyond our personal benefit. There can be no upward mobility, if rampant self-hatred, animosity, and strife persists in our community.

Saving and building our sons, goes beyond a photo opportunity and a motivational speech. It begins with recognizing that our brothers have value and they have something to offer the world. If your mind is only confined to negative and stereotypical media portrayals of our brothers, then you will never do anything to unearth their greatness.

In order to effectively transform someone's life, you

have to see beyond where they are and empower them for where they can be. It takes visionaries to engage in this work. The value that you see in them, can be instilled in them. The value leads to love, providing access, and opportunities, via the parameters of commitment. There can be no commitment without trust.

How many promises have been made to you, that somebody broke? How did that impact your life? So many times people have promised us things, only to renege on their word which ultimately lowered our expectation. When you stop expecting, it limits the parameters of living your best life.

Your level of commitment, goes beyond color and background, it speaks to the aspect of having a heart to love and lead with courage. If you're only focused on what's in it for me, how can you help someone get anything out of life? Real brotherhood does more than compete, it's about helping your brother complete their vision and bring it to fruition. In order to save and build, we have to seize the moment. There's no better time than now, to answer the call.

I AM...MY BROTHER'S KEEPER!

CHAPTER 2

By Any Means Necessary

In order to impact the next generation, we have to strategize, mobilize, and organize an action plan to create an intergenerational transfer of wealth and wisdom. It's incumbent upon us, to do more than pass down a Gucci belt, Air Jordan sneakers, or True Religion Jeans to the next generation. We have to do more, than be consumers of material possessions. We must become investors, in the lives of our brothers.

DIRTY HANDS

The poignant and quaint four word phrase, *By Any Means Necessary*, was originally coined by a French playwright, Jean-Paul Sartre in his theatrical play, *Dirty Hands*. The script detailed a killer's motives and the execution of his mission. The play was not focused on who did it, but the focus was on why it was done.

Sartre's four word phrase, *By Any Means Necessary* matriculated into the English lexicon, during the Civil Rights era. It commenced through a speech, from a man formerly known as "Detroit Red" with the birth name of Malcolm Little. He is better known to the world, as Malcolm X. He spoke those iconic words, at the Organization of the Afro-American Unity's Founding Rally, on June 28th, 1964.

If Jean-Paul Sartre, the writer of the play *Dirty Hands*, was alive today, I would say to him, "Isn't it interesting that America, has those same dirty hands?" It's the hands that are riddled with the blood, of the "hellacaust" that drowned 10 million African bodies, in the Atlantic Ocean, during the Trans-Atlantic slave trade. America's hands have blood on them, because of the countless lynchings of Black bodies "swingin' in the southern breeze, blood on the leaves, hanging from the poplar trees." Those lyrics provide the substratum to the sentiments, that Billie Holiday and Nina Simone so poignantly, mellifluously, and melodiously echoed about in the song *Strange Fruit*.

America your hands are dirty, because you assassinated many of the greatest leaders, of the 20th century. Martin, Malcolm, and Medgar in the 1960s. America has dirty hands, because of the disproportionate warehousing of Black males in the prison system. This in fact, commenced during Reaganomics and the pseudo "War on Drugs" of the 1980s, which has risen to astronomical heights in our times of this New Jim Crow era.

BACK TO THE FUTURE

No, we cannot forget because we do not live in the "United States of Amnesia." Yet, we must make America aware, that its hands are still dirty, from the brutal hate crime killing of Emmett Till in 1955. Ever since the tyrannical murder of Emmet Till, I'm beginning to believe that time travel is real. Marty McFly and Doc Brown cannot rescue us, from the horror film version of *Back To The Future*. Simply because it seems, as if little has changed. Yes, we're living in times of breakthroughs in technology, but there are tremendous breakdowns in our community.

Before Dr. King's assassination in 1968, he prophetically warned us, about the triple evils of society (poverty, racism, and militarism). These evils thwart the spectrum of brotherhood, to build beloved the community. Where is the beloved community, that will embrace our brothers?

As we reside in these yet to be United States of America, we are living in times where every 28 hours, a Black male is the victim of police brutality. Police shootings, have become modern day lynchings. Our society has transitioned from "hands up don't shoot" to "comply or die." You can be unarmed and still deemed dangerous.

What we cannot do, is simply glance at the upheaval of racism that America produced, by letting it off the hook. For indeed, it cannot sanitize its "dirty hands" from the stains of the blood, that was shed by countless Black men and women, who symbolize the giants on whose shoulders we stand today.

We find ourselves living in troubled times, from the city of Ferguson, Missouri to Charleston, South Carolina to Baltimore, Maryland and Detroit, Michigan. The fight for freedom, justice, and equality continues because it has yet to be realized, in these divided states of America. We must continue to pursue liberty, in the face of injustice for all that are oppressed and afflicted. The poor Whites, indigenous Native Americans, Hispanic/Latino community, Asian Americans, and those maligned in the Black community.

GRADUATE TO THE NEXT LEVEL

Oliver Wendell Holmes, a noted author and physician, declared "A mind stretched by new ideas, never returns to its original dimension." When you begin to stretch your mind and build your faith, then the parameters of your life exponentially expand as a result. I've got breaking news for you and that is, you can't graduate to the next level, by thinking small and surrounding yourself with small minded people. It's incumbent upon you to understand that, you can never expect people with limited thinking, to understand your unlimited dreams! Simply because, if your dreams are affordable, then you're not dreaming BIG enough!

MY BROTHER'S KEEPER - DR. EDDIE M. CONNOR, JR.

Graduating to the next level, isn't only about being celebrated, it's about being dedicated in every area of your life. Graduating to the next level, is about more than being "liked" on Facebook. It's about studying, by putting your face in a book. It isn't about how many people, are following you on Twitter. It's about where you're leading those, who follow you. It isn't about, how many likes you get on Instagram. It's about how much love you can show, to the common man. At the end of the day, it's not about accepting awards and receiving applause, it's about working together for a cause!

No longer can we have a generation of young people, who have style but lack substance. On the iPhone listening to the rapper 2 Chainz and rocking two chains on their neck, but lacking heart. Listening to Drake and Future, but unwilling to work to build their future. No longer can we have young ladies, who strut in high heels but have low standards and self-esteem. Sisters who "twerk," but refuse to work. Brothers who rock high top designer shoes, but have low ambition. If we pull up their sagging communities, sagging goals, sagging homes, and sagging dreams, I guarantee our brothers, will pull up their sagging grades and sagging pants.

We have become materialistic purchasing cars, clothes, bags, and wearing chains, but failing to understand the sacrifices of our forefathers and mothers who were whipped and locked in chains. In this ultra celebrity driven culture, we must understand that the real role models are not Beyonce, Rihanna, Nicki Minaj, Jeezy, Weezy, Yeezy, and Jay-Z. The real role models, are still you and me!

We can't stretch to the next level, if we are stifled by the opinions of other people. If you can't handle criticism, then you're surely not ready for success. In this life, you have to realize that there will be critics, cynics, naysayers, and haters. In spite of it, you have to use them all as elevators, to escalate to the next level. Use every hater, to make yourself and others greater. The people that you surround yourself with and the lessons you learn, should enhance your growth not stunt it!

LEARN, LEAD, AND GROW

Psychologists suggest that we learn in three ways, via observation, experimentation, and maturation. There are certain things, you learn by watching through observation and others you learn by doing via experimentation. Then there are certain lessons forged through the pain of growing through, by definition of experience through maturation.

In this life, you can't get to the next level, without growing through some stuff. By definition, there is no anesthetic, to take to avoid the pain of growth. You can't numb yourself and wake up after being unconscious, to find out that all of your problems are now solved. The lessons of life, cause you to endure the process of maturity and self-development. On your path to purpose, you will feel every bit of shaking and stretching, which transforms you into a better you. Yes, it's true that only the strong survive, but only the strongest will thrive! We have to empower our brothers with the message, that God didn't build you to break. You were built to breakthrough and become the best you, that you can be.

The life of our sainted ancestors tells us, there are certain lessons in the valley, that you can't learn on the mountaintop. You must remember everything you learned in the valley, on your climb to the mountaintop. If you develop amnesia, because of your achievement then you will be right back in that same valley, until you learn the lesson.

LEADERSHIP ON THE LINE

The reason that you've labored and learned, is so that you can be qualified to lead. Real leadership, is not about how many followers you create. The essence of real leadership, is about how many leaders you create. Real leaders, birth leaders. I'm a living witness, that you can't teach anybody anything, who thinks they know everything. Simply because, a know-it-all really knows nothing at all. We must be open to listen and learn, from each other and the previous generation, in order so that we can lead effectively. It's one thing to share what you know, it's another thing to share what people need to know. Great leadership is not determined, by what you do in good times. Great leadership is determined, by how you respond, in challenging times.

This speaks to the essence, of technical versus adaptive change, expressed in the book *Leadership On The Line* (Heifetz, Linsky). The aspect of technical change is only surface, but adaptive change is substantive because it goes to the root of the problem to bring transformation. You can't bring adaptive change, without having one foot in the problem and one foot in the solution. Adaptive change in our schools, churches, communities, and the lives of our brothers speaks to a higher calling. You have to be able to discern the pulse of the people, by breathing life into those comatose and desensitized, to the struggles we face.

CURRENCY OR BANKRUPTCY

You can sit and learn all day, but it's what you do with the information, when you get up that matters. Your mind is a bank and the information you learn is currency. The power of knowledge becomes like money, that you can use when you apply it. Essentially, the more knowledge that you gain, the more you have to use and share.

If there is no information, there will be no mental currency. As a result, no currency leads to bankruptcy. This is why, we are in the trenches of not just a digital divide, in society, but an intergenerational divide. Simply because, there is a lack of informational currency, that being wealth and wisdom being transferred to our children.

Scripture declares, "My people are destroyed, for lack of knowledge" (Hosea 4:6). It's a lack of wisdom and informational currency. Simply because informational currency makes you a visionary, but without a vision, the people will perish (Proverbs 29:18). If you have sight but no vision, then you're still blind! Wearing the finest eye glass frames will enhance your sight, but not your vision. The power of vision goes beyond your eyes, it's discerned in your heart. Without a vision you're just existing, rather than living. If you have a vision, then you can expect provision.

Sir Isaac Newton stated, "I see further, by standing

on the shoulders of giants." Don't let the pain of your past, blind you from the greatness of your future. You are here today, because you're standing on the shoulders, of those who have come before you. Their testimony, to fight against oppression should propel you forward, to persevere beyond any odd or obstacle. Your motto must be, "Forward ever and backward never" by any means necessary!

I AM...MY BROTHER'S KEEPER!

CHAPTER 3

Freedom Ain't Free

Our lives serve as a stark reminder, that freedom costs us something. Indeed it's evident that "Freedom ain't free" and it comes with a price. As long as terrorism and tyranny, racism and rage, continue to pervade in our churches and communities, we must continue to fight!

The Civil Rights icon, Fannie Lou Hamer suggested, "We did not sing we shall overcome, so that when we overcame, we forgot about those who still need to come over." I propose to you, have we forgot about the least, the left out, the lost, the overlooked, the underserved, and those underrepresented in our communities?

We have eclipsed the 50th year of the enactment of

the Voting Rights Act of 1965. More than just voter registration, we need voter education for the protection of our rights and privileges. Former chairman of the NAACP and freedom fighter, Julian Bond declared, "Good things don't come to those who wait, they come to those who agitate." Have you become so cynical and desensitized to violence, impoverished communities, unemployment, mass incarceration, and lack of opportunities for our brothers and sisters, that you refuse to agitate the system and speak truth to power?

BARK AND NO BITE

In the shadows of Julian Bond and Amelia Boynton Robinson, the question is who will pick up the baton now to run this race? The time for posturing is over. You can't look like a lion and sound like a kitten. You can't dogmatically bark and have no bite. The bite is in the fight. As we protest, we must engender transformative policies and principles. We're losing too many of our brothers. The time has come that we must say, "If you're not going to fight with me on the front lines, then don't get in my way. Go and stand on the sidelines."

FOR APPLAUSE OR A CAUSE?

Life is not about living for applause, it's about uplifting someone else for a unique cause. The real revolutionary rap lyrics suggested, "If I can help somebody as I pass along. If I can cheer somebody with a word or song, then my living shall not be in vain." Is there not a cause?

EDUCATION OR INCARCERATION

We are the talented tenth, that must invest into the ninety of society, in efforts to transform our culture, classrooms, and communities that are in crisis. Look around you, our culture, classrooms, and communities are in upheaval. The resounding question would suggest, what is the value of our lives in America? The school system would express, approximately $7,500 per pupil expenditure. However, the prison system would calculate $35,000 as America, has the largest prison population in the world.

More and more, we are clearly seeing, that it's either education or incarceration. When will we get tired and upset enough, to "get off our duff" and disrupt the preschool-to-prison pipeline? At an astounding rate, they are closing our schools, but the prisons remain open.

FROM ANGER TO ACTION

James Baldwin, a leading novelist during the Harlem Renaissance affirmed, "To be Black in America and to be relatively conscious, is to be in a rage almost all the time." Simply because, there is righteous indignation throughout the streets and nation. How can you not be angered and enraged, when you see the mistreatment of our brothers?

We must develop an organized structure, to transform our destructive anger, into constructive action.

UNITED NOT DIVIDED

In the Black community, we are often like fingers that are divided, simply poking at problems. Yes, we are doing great things separately, but imagine what we can do cohesively and collectively.

The crippling effects, of the "Willie Lynch" philosophy and "Post Traumatic Slave Syndrome," has kept us in a state of distrust of one another. It has kept us divided, rather than united. If we can ever bring our fingers together and become like a fist, we will see victory in our community. When we bring our gifts, assets, and resources together, then we will see transformative progression. When we are united, we can address drug abuse, poverty, education, incarceration, and mental health issues.

Indeed and in fact, a brother is born for adversity. Not to cause it or leave you in it, but to help you overcome it. We have operated in disunity, division, and disorganization for far too long, by design.

Scripture declares, "A house divided against itself, cannot stand" (Mark 3:25). Our community has operated, being separated like fingers far too long. We are doing great things separately, but teamwork makes the dream work and we're stronger when we become like a fist. For 400 years, they have sought to keep us separated, because the oppressor understood the power of unity.

We will only be able to clean up our communities, build our brothers, stabilize our schools, reduce unemployment and incarceration, if we work together. It's true that "Coming together is a beginning, keeping together is progress, but working together is success."

When we come together like a fist, we can knockout

violence. When we become like a fist, we can knockout poverty. We can knockout the high school dropout rate. We can knockout drug abuse. It's time to fight the good fight of faith! Dr. King affirmed, "Freedom is never voluntarily given by the oppressor; it must be demanded by the oppressed."

Malcolm X declared, "Nobody can give you freedom. Nobody can give you equality, justice, or anything. If you're a man, take it." We must place a demand, on the freedom we desire! We must man up. We must take our rightful place, as leaders in our homes and communities which will bring fruitful change.

DIVERSITY IS NOT ADVERSITY

We must bridge our differences and embrace the power of our diversity to learn from one another, grow together, and overcome every adversity. We must discover strength in diversity, rather than weakness and adversity in diversity.

Our diversity should unite us, not divide us. Our communities, are at an intersection and it's either education or incarceration. Maybe not physically, but it can be a psychological imprisonment. Most people go through their day, physically awake but mentally asleep and unconscious.

The tragedy is to breathe life, but never live it. Some of us are only physically alive, but spiritually dead. Many people are merely existing, but not living. According to author Mark Twain, "The two most important days in your life, is the day you were born and the day you find out why."

The WHY symbolizes your purpose within. The fact that you're alive, in this present moment reflects the fact that you have a purpose. It's up to you, to understand the enormity of your purpose, so you can live with purpose, on purpose, and for a purpose...because you have a dynamic purpose!

You have a God given gift and purpose, that is uniquely yours. It can't be duplicated or imitated. You have to discover it and use it to inspire the world. No dream is unreachable, no vision is unachievable, and no goal is unattainable.

It's not just what you go through, it's how you handle what you go through. There are certain things in life, that you must GROW through. The greater the pain, the greater your promise and purpose. The greater the battle, the greater your breakthrough and blessing.

The commitment and love that our predecessors exuded in the fight for freedom, should encourage us to pick up the baton and fight for future generations. It will cost, but the price is worth the return on its investment!

I AM...MY BROTHER'S KEEPER!

CHAPTER 4

Literacy Is Key - (Boys 2 Books)

T he old adage suggests, "If you want to hide something from a Black person, put it in a book." It seems like we live in the "United States of Amnesia" because we fail to remember, that more than 200 years ago, it was illegal for Black people to read. If caught reading, you would be maimed or lynched. This brutal practice took place, because the oppressor knew that education was the death of mental slavery. In so doing, if the psychological chains came off, then the physical chains would be broken as well.

Malcolm X declared, "The ability to read, awoke inside me some long dormant craving, to be mentally alive." We are seeing a growing epidemic of brothers, who are physically alive, but mentally asleep. Walking zombies in our communities, with no zeal.

THE ILLS OF ILLITERACY

Universal literacy is a prime necessity, in order to compete in a global economy. The following are statistics, according to the National Institute for Literacy:

- 42 Million American adults cannot read.

- 50 Million adults are unable to read, higher than a fourth or fifth grade level.

- Only 11 percent of Black males, in the fourth grade, read at/or above a fourth grade level.

- 85 percent of all juvenile offenders, rate as functionally or marginally illiterate.

- 20 percent of high school seniors can be classified, as being functionally illiterate at the time they graduate.

- 70 percent of US prisoners are classified as illiterate.

- 43 percent of people who live below the poverty line, are functionally illiterate.

NEW JIM CROW

There is a frightening statistic that suggests, "If a child has not mastered reading by first grade, they have less than a 20 percent chance to graduate from high school." The ever-present connection between illiteracy and incarceration, continues to fester as an academic abscess. This connection is systematically structured, to keep our brothers on a modern day plantation, known as the prison-industrial complex. Dr. Jawanza Kunjufu in his book, *Countering the Conspiracy to Destroy Black Boys,* asserts that "Prisons are built, based on third grade reading scores." This data determines future occupancy, in prison facilities.

For any business to be successful, there must be a gauge to determine profitability and sustainability. The school-to-prison pipeline of third grade reading scores, is that primary gauge. Guess who the target is?

Unfortunately, our Black and Hispanic brothers are

in the crosshairs of a cultural chasm. The remnants of Jim Crow did not die, it just multiplied into a new version of mass incarceration, inequality in education, gentrification, etc.

The National Commission on Adult Literacy suggests, "Illiteracy is highly correlated with imprisonment, given that 56 percent of U.S. adults in prison or jail, were deemed to have very low literacy skills." The same money that is put into prisons, needs to be invested into teaching our brothers to read.

ENABLED OR CRIPPLED

I have been an educator for more than a decade, teaching in the high school classroom and on the college campus. The teaching profession is one of the most maligned, underpaid, and undervalued in America. I realize that I make up, only 2 percent of Black male teachers in the

United States. Indeed we are scarce, in the school system. When we get out of school, we stay out of schools. I believe much of it stems from the adverse treatment, we received, when we were students in school. Since the age of 18, I have personally dedicated my life and time, to inspire our youth to succeed.

Public education, is primarily the immersion of middle class White women and poor Black boys. Are White female teachers, afraid of Black males? If that be the case, how can you properly instruct, who you are afraid of? Are today's classrooms, culturally competent enough, to engage a diverse generation of students?

In comparison, to any other time in American history, our students are more culturally diverse, than ever before. However, the diverse demographics of our student population, fails to reflect in our teacher population. Researchers suggest that 83 percent, of America's teachers, are White. The majority are female. Furthermore, 7 percent of teachers are Hispanic and 2 percent are Hispanic males. Among teachers, 6 percent are Black. Only 2 percent, are Black males. Are students at a disadvantage, because they rarely experience Black and Hispanic male teachers, in the classroom? Regrettably, most of our students, will never see a teacher in the classroom, who looks like me.

In a White female dominated system of academia, improving the education of Black boys, begins with them being taught by Black and Hispanic men.

Beyond race, the expectation that teachers have of students is the demarcating factor, as to whether a child will fail or succeed. Teachers must raise their expectations, rather than lower their standards. Jamal can learn, just as well as Johnny. Keisha can learn, just as well as Katie. Learning differently, does not equate to deficiency.

When we believe that our students can learn and

succeed, it will encourage them to believe, that they too can succeed. We cannot afford to have cultural cataracts. Rather, we must put on our learning lens, in order to see the value in our students, which they are often blind to themselves.

When teachers have high expectations for our students, it helps to enhance the level of achievement among our students. When we believe that our brothers and sisters can thrive and overcome, it will encourage them to persevere. Expectations, time on task, and classroom management are significant factors to the success of our youth in school.

Our communities and churches must offer academic enrichment programs, whether or not they are government funded. We must keep our libraries and schools open. We need mentors, literacy advocates, parents, and strong males to invest in the lives of our youth.

The changing dynamics of education and bureaucracy,

oftentimes cripple our children from exercising their inner genius. Within the classroom, especially working with boys, many of our young men close their eyes when they open a book. I often wondered, as to why this underwhelming phenomenon would happen, time and time again?

As I engaged in my graduate work, my focus was on boys and literacy challenges. In so doing, I began to see the connection, between illiteracy and incarceration. We often say, "boys hate to read" and ask the question, why don't boys like reading? I would suggest, in fact that is not always the case. Yes, researchers suggest that by the time boys enter ninth grade, 50 percent consider themselves non-readers. Why is this happening?

ACT LIKE A GIRL?

The indictment is not on the boys, per se. Rather, it's on

how we instruct, how we raise, and what we give our boys. As you have read thus far, you can surmise that I'm not interested in being politically correct. The reality is America wants boys, to behave like girls in the classroom. They want boys to be prim, proper, quiet, and engaged in little to no movement. In fact, boys are the total opposite. I have worked with boys, in every age and stage of their developmental years. Regardless of race, there are more similarities than differences.

There are three critical grades for Black boys, which impact their education: kindergarten, fourth grade, and ninth grade. In kindergarten, boys are excited to learn and sit in the front of the classroom. In fourth grade, the landscape of literacy shifts. As a result, reading levels begin to decline. If boys can't read proficiently, by the end of fourth grade, jail is projected to be their destination.

Prior to fourth grade, boys learn to read. After fourth

grade, boys read to learn. Prior to fourth grade, work is collaborative. After fourth grade, work becomes individualized.

When young brothers enter ninth grade, the disinterest level toward school, is at an all time high. Boys prefer to sit in the back of the classroom, desire to "look cool" and many drop out.

Boys and girls learn differently. Education is primarily constructed, to cater to girls instead of boys. Research suggests that girls generally mature, on average, three years quicker than boys. As a result, they have a longer attention span and have a greater tolerance to remain in their seats. This doesn't mean that boys are defective or deficient, it just means that boys and girls are different.

Boys are innately aggressive, competitive, jovial, and inquisitive. When is masculinity ever applauded in the classroom? When is mental toughness ever celebrated?

The more docile the behavior, the better one is looked upon. The more subservient the student, the better we see them as in the classroom. If you show weakness, you are praised. If you show strength, you are shunned. Who makes it cool, for boys to learn in our schools? Are we sending the message to our boys, that if you want to succeed in education, then do what the girls do? Essentially, act like a girl? To be demonized and criticized in the classroom and community, is perplexing enough.

In no way, am I saying that boys should have freedom, to act like "hooligans" in a classroom or home. Trust and believe, it didn't happen in my classroom. By any means necessary, I'm not giving you a license to let it happen in your school or home for that matter.

However, my approach with boys comes from the spectrum that I've been their age before. I understand their energy, but I show them how to harness that power. It's like being a Marvel Comics character, endowed with a superpower, which can be used to help or hurt someone. Your power can be used to create or destroy. We have to show our boys how to use their "powers" to benefit themselves and others. You can't do that, without establishing positive relationships with our young brothers.

IT DOESN'T "ADD" UP

When the education system doesn't know, how to corral one's level of energy, what do they do? In fact they medicate, sedate, tranquilize, and throw boys into an "educational jail," called "special education." We have technical terms, for the energetic ones and call it, *Attention Deficit Disorder (ADD)* or *Attention Deficit Hyperactivity Disorder (ADHD)*. However, it doesn't always "ADD" up.

What is so special, about "special education?" Now, of course there is a caveat and that is some students, do need special education services or medicine to harness their attention/skill set. However, most are improperly diagnosed. Albeit, the right instruction, that caters to their multiple intelligences will cause students to thrive in an environment, that unlocks their unique abilities.

Boys are active by nature and are more prone to be diagnosed with ADHD and medicated than girls. Even despite race, boys are more likely to be placed in special education than girls. If boys refuse to cooperate, then schools begin to medicate.

According to the National Education Association, "Black boys are more likely than their peers, to be placed in special education classes, labeled mentally retarded, suspended from school, or drop out altogether." They are also less likely, to be enrolled in honors classes or gifted and talented programs.

More than any other ethnicity or gender, we are

witnessing special education, overmedication, and the under education of Black boys in the American school system. Black boys are the most mistreated, maligned, exploited, and underserved child population in America. Instead of education, we have settled for medication, rather than mediation and drugging over disciplining.

Thank God, that my high school guidance counselor, was not my classroom teacher. Surely, she would have seen fit to medicate me and place me in special education. The right instruction, care, commitment, and concern can transform a struggling student, into a successfully academic student leader. It can take someone, who is classified as "learning disabled" to learning enabled. I have engaged in the work and seen it with my own eyes!

CRP IS THE NEW CPR

There is an instruction module, *CRP: Culturally Relevant Pedagogy*. This concept relates to the cultural competence and an instructors skill at teaching, in a cross-cultural or multicultural setting. More than ever, our students are culturally diverse, yet our teachers reflect homogeneity. The students are changing, but the teachers and education system, remains archaic and stagnant.

Why don't schools teach Black History and Hispanic History, throughout the course of the school year? Why is it only relegated, to one day or a month (if that)? In order to have true competency in a classroom, you have to incorporate one's cultural history. This must be interwoven, into state standards and classroom curriculum.

The CRP concept, is CPR for diverse classrooms. It breathes life, into the lives of students. Teachers must be metacognitive and ask critical questions: "How do I engage diverse students, who don't look or think like me? How do I engage students, who don't come from where I'm from? How do I engage those, who use language in a way, that I don't?" These questions must be addressed, in order to provide sustainability in your school and classroom community.

For many of our brothers and sisters, life is a tough teacher. In essence, life gives them a test before the lesson. No father in the home, family members incarcerated, and many are raising themselves. Oftentimes, we don't realize that our students didn't eat dinner last night and they didn't have breakfast this morning. Over the weekend, their sister died or their cousin, was killed in a rage of violence. Our culture, community, classroom, and curriculum is in crisis.

Education is a life or death situation. It's either education or mass incarceration, for our youth. We have to not only save them, but we have to provide intangible tools to build them for the future.

The substratum of great mentoring and teaching, begins with developing and cultivating positive relationships. For any relationship to be fruitful, you have to forge and foster enduring connections. Find a common thread of interest with students. Our young people are in search of authenticity, honesty, integrity, and connectivity. They just want to know if you notice them, love them, and will speak a word of encouragement to them.

As leaders in the classroom and community, we know how to discipline, but do we have a receptive ear to listen? You can't effectively teach, who you don't know. You can only dwell, according to knowledge. We have to know not only our students learning style, but we should have knowledge of their lifestyle.

We can't make stereotypical assertions and judgments about our youth. We can't base their greatness on negative media perceptions, how they wear their pants, or their family background. It doesn't matter how tough our youth portray themselves to be, all of them have a "fragile, do not drop" label on their lives. They don't care how much you know, until they know how much you care. We must handle our youth with care. We must roll up our sleeves and dig deeper into the trenches, because our youth are falling through the cracks.

CULTURAL CATARACTS

Teachers must take precautions, to ensure that they don't develop cultural cataracts in our classrooms. This happens, when you only see our youth, through a skewed lens. Diversity speaks to the fact, that our students are different, but they are not deficient.

The Aristotelian deduction, syllogistic reasoning, and critical thinking skills that our students possess within differs, but is not a deficit. When we hone in on it, to possess a panoramic perspective, it engenders within us 20/20 vision. This clear spectrum of vision empowers us, to look beyond where our students are, and see them for where they can be. We are ebullient, as we open our mouths to teach and speak. However, we should also be receptive, to open our ears to learn and listen.

MENTALLY TRUANT

I see you everyday, but I know nothing about you. Why should someone learn from you, if you refuse to listen and learn from them? How many students across America, show up each day to class and are physically present, but mentally absent?

We are bombastic about cracking down on physical truancy, but what are we doing to combat mental truancy? Holistic education and teaching the whole child, goes beyond raising test scores and meeting AYP (Adequate Yearly Progress). What are we doing to raise the level of a student's thinking, their character, and help them to progress in life? When we begin to change our approach, the standards we set will be met, because we are meeting the needs of students.

Four E's to achieve A's and B's

The greatest indicator of student success, is the belief that students can succeed! Believing in our youth, motivates them to believe in themselves. We can't expect our brothers to be determined, if we see them as deficient, from a deficit model. There are four key components, that promote success for students:

1. Environment - Develop a culture that promotes literacy and leadership for young learners, using culturally relevant materials.

2. Engagement - True classroom and community leaders pay attention, to what motivates and engages students to learn. Incorporate the multiple intelligences and learning modalities. Students learn in a variety of ways. Target your auditory, kinesthetic, and visual learners.

3. Expectations - Believe that students can succeed. Allow students to have autonomy, in setting goals for themselves.

A classroom that invokes character, commitment, and cooperation between a teacher and students, will reap positive benefits.

4. Encouragement - These leaders pay attention, to what motivates and engages youth to learn. They provide positive reinforcement as a result. Motivation and encouragement, must be the driving force, especially for reluctant learners. Incorporate information, instruction, and inspiration.

BOOKS AND VALUES

The quest of culturally relevant pedagogy, is quite significant in the aspect of literacy development. The late Walter Dean Myers, a prolific author of more than 100 books declared, "Books transmit values, if I'm not in the book what does that say about my value?" Myers, calls us into question about the information, we place in the hands of children.

Researchers suggest, that the average 14-year-old checks their social media page at least 100 times per day. Another suggests, by the time a young person is 18-years-old, they have played an average of 10,000 hours of video games. What would happen, if our young people logged out of Facebook (Instagram or Twitter) and spent more time with their face in a book?

WAKA FLOCKA & W.E.B.

There is much work to do, when our young people know more about Waka Flocka Flame, than they do about W.E.B. Du Bois. We can't sit back and let BET, MTV, entertainers, athletes, and celebrities raise our children. We have to step up and assume responsibility, as their parents, teachers, mentors, and advocates.

According to my former Professor, Dr. Vivian Johnson, "Literacy is threefold." You relate the text-to-text, text-to-self, and the text-to-world. A reading text doesn't come alive, until the reader connects personal experiences with it, to exact meaning from it. Unless it has meaning to you, it's just text with black words on white paper. What is our students' cultural frame of reference? What is their prior knowledge, of relating one book to the other, connecting it to themselves, or their world?

IRC, STEM, MELTS

An Integrated Reading Curriculum (IRC), must be infused in our classrooms. The power of multidisciplinary integration, provides real world connections, to culturally relevant content/themes presented. The blueprint for broad based curriculum literacy, must be school and nationwide.

Education places a primary focus on Science, Technology, Engineering, and Mathematics (STEM). However, STEM needs an educational facelift. It's transitionary concept must infuse literacy. The concept of Mathematics, Engineering, Literacy, Technology, and Science (MELTS) must be immersed. Not that one is greater than the other, but they all work cohesively together.

ENRICH THROUGH LITERACY

Frederick Douglass declared, "Once you learn to read, you will be forever free." The following, provide tips to enrich your home, classroom, and community using literacy tools, to build our brothers.

1. Provide culturally relevant literature books in classrooms, communities, and barber shops to develop reading comprehension, verb conjugation, and literacy acquisition skills.

2. Provide texts that are challenging, meaningful, and engaging. Promote discussion and literacy circles.

3. Use computers/technology devices, review articles, download e-books, word games/apps (i.e. Wattpad)

4. Incorporate reading/writing strategies, throughout content area instruction.

5. Expose students to diverse authors and content.

THE ACHIEVEMENT GAP

The profound leader and educator, Mary McLeod Bethune, affirmed "The whole world opened to me, when I learned to read." The achievement gap that is exacerbated in school, primarily begins at home. Literacy development closes the gap, illiteracy widens it.

The National Center for Education Statistics, detailed the average hours spent on homework per week. Asian children study 10.3 hours, White children study 6.8 hours, Hispanic children study 6.4 hours, and Black children average 6.3 hours per week.

The average Black child spends 38 hours per week, watching TV (Tunnel Vision), texting, playing video games, surfing the internet, and/or listening to music. We must place a time frame on the TV, video games, and other media forms, that our children are engaged in, which take precedence over their academics. We must be as eager to be informed, as we are to be entertained.

Time on task and expectations, can close the achievement gap. The odds stacked against someone, never prevented them from achieving via self-motivation and mentoring. I tell my young brothers, "The only time play comes before work, is in a dictionary." Success will not be experienced without sacrifice.

According to linguists, the average pre-literacy exposure for White children, is approximately 4,000 hours. On the contrary, for Black children is only 350 hours. Children from high-income families are exposed to 30 million more words, than children from low-income homes. Before our children even pick up a book or step foot in school, there is already a gap. Certain children have already began the race to the top, before others have even stepped into the arena. We must open the parachute of our children's minds, with rich literature for their development.

Marian Wright Edelman of the Children's Defense Fund, is a leading advocate and activist for disadvantaged children. Edelman asserts, "A majority of all children and more than 76 percent, or more of fourth and eighth grade Black and Hispanic public school students, cannot read or compute at grade level." Indeed many of our children are confined to a cradle-to-prison pipeline, due to low literacy levels and low expectations. The spectrum of prolonged low levels of literacy, limits our children to homeless and jobless futures.

THE BLAME GAME

The New York Times reported, that only 12 percent of fourth grade Black boys are reading on grade level. Conversely, what is being done to help the 88 percent below grade level? I have mentored and developed the literacy skills, of our brothers who have been passed through school, but can't read a sentence. Regrettably, they are sitting in ninth grade, with a third grade reading level. Then the questions come, "Why is this kid acting out? Why is he angry, irrational, and emotionally disturbed in the classroom?" It's because the people who were entrusted to raise and teach him, failed him! You better believe he's angry, because life is passing by and he realizes that he's unprepared for the real world.

We have transitioned from the concept of "No Child Left Behind" to the harsh reality, that most children are behind. Time and time again, our brothers/sons, are passed on to somebody else and we wash our hands of them, as if it isn't our problem.

So, everybody is pointing fingers at each other and playing the blame game. "It's the parents' fault. It's the teachers' fault. It's the administrators' fault. It's the rappers, it's the media, and it's the community." No, it's YOU! It's your inability to accept responsibility, for who has been entrusted into your hands.

When you mentor and teach, in a community center or classroom setting and begin to see that child as yours, you will invest yourself into that child. Many bad teachers have wrecked our children's outlook on education. All it takes is one good teacher, to see greatness in a child and lift them higher.

Who will step up and repair the breach? Who will provide breakthroughs, when things are broken? Who will save, not "this kid" or "those kids" but OUR kids? This is OUR future, these are OUR children, and OUR brothers!

BOYS 2 BOOKS

This is why I developed my literacy and mentoring program, *Boys 2 Books*. Simply because I was tired of passing the buck. I was tired of seeing our brothers burn in an academic hell, when nobody would extinguish the flames. The more information I gained through study and the more knowledgeable I became, the greater my responsibility was to my classroom and community.

I decided to develop a book club, at my school twice per week, specifically for boys. I saw this as an opportunity to speak to younger versions of myself. I never had a personal mentor, older brother, or much less a father growing up, and I wanted to give young brothers what I didn't have.

Did I wave books down the hall, beckoning guys to come after school? Heck no! The bait I used was movies, hip-hop, motivational speakers, sports, and the major draw…FOOD! In order to teach people, you have to reach them where they are first.

As I developed *Boys 2 Books* in Metro Detroit, my vision was to reduce the illiteracy rate in the city, disrupt the school-to-prison pipeline, and stimulate a love for reading in the lives of our boys and young men. Did I tell them that using technical verbiage? No. Did I exemplify it in a relatable way? Yes!

Literacy, Leadership, Life Skills

Boys 2 Books, is designed to expand opportunities for success and advance the achievement of boys and young men via literacy, leadership, and life skills enrichment.

This literacy/mentorship program equips and empowers youth via self-awareness, self-esteem, and self-respect that fosters personal development and community involvement. *Boys 2 Books* is a nationally recognized mentoring program, which entails improving reading levels, developing reading skills, empowering boys and young men via culturally relevant rich literature. Culturally relevant books are used as a bridge, to help boys and young men increase their reading proficiency.

Literacy tests and strategies are provided, to develop phonemic awareness, language acquisition, and reading comprehension skills. Boys and young men actively engage in dialogue, keep journals, and are given methods in which to practice life skills. Much of the life skill training involves professionalism in the workplace, job interviews, professional attire, self-respect, personal hygiene, developing positive relationships, academic excellence, etiquette, college readiness, and community responsibility.

Boys 2 Books is designed to unlock the purpose and potential, that resides in the lives of our boys and young men. Our young brothers are exposed to community resources via influential leaders, career development, field trips, and information to empower them on the road to success.

I genuinely desire to help our brothers, become better readers, thinkers, and leaders. Our young men already have the intangibles for success. Many of them don't realize it, but you can help them to identify it. **As you can see, the *Boys 2 Books* program is needed in your school district, youth program, community center, etc.**

READING IS FUNDAMENTAL

I hear it all the time, from many of the boys I mentor, "Dr. C. I don't like to read." I actually love to hear that, because it gives me an opportunity to engage our brothers and discover their core interests. When you adapt your style and become more than a sage on the stage, to being a guide on the side, that's when you learn how children think.

The greatest teachers of our children, are those who are willing to learn from our children. When you discover the interest of a child and develop positive relationships, they become more receptive to your message and method of instruction.

I began to probe and discover, why boys don't like to

read. The resounding answer, yielded the fact that many books lack cultural implications. The material isn't applicable to their lives. Many boys are interested in reading books that evoke action, mystery, history, sports, science, and fiction.

If they don't like to read, but their favorite sports star is LeBron James, then what should you do? Yes, give that young brother a book about NBA player, LeBron James. I have never seen it fail, for a young man to pick up that book to read it. This is also a good indicator, to find out if he is struggling to read the book. It's a great way to engage reluctant learners, or those who need literacy reinforcement strategies. Do our young people, need to develop fundamental reading skills? Absolutely!

Our brothers have entertainment and sports dreams of grandeur. Mainly because, that is what they are exposed to the most. We must expose them to greater career opportunities, not narrow ones. As we encourage our brothers to pursue their dreams of entertainment/athletics, we must also tell them to have a plan b. The plan "b" should begin with a book! Genuine mentors and instructors, help them to discover the FUN in fundamental.

You may never do a math problem, to solve a pythagorean theorem. You may never have to decipher physics or understand the constructs of potential and kinetic energy. You may not have to reach through the annals of time, to understand the Greco-Roman traditions in cultural history. You may never have to understand an adjectival clause, or be intoxicated with the exuberance of your verbosity. However, you will have to read every single day, for the rest of your life. Basic literacy skills are fundamental, to the success of our brothers.

I AM...MY BROTHER'S KEEPER!

CHAPTER 5

Education or Mass Incarceration

Hosea 4:6 declares, "My people are destroyed for lack of knowledge." Our youth are dropping out of school, violence and crime is sky rocketing, communities are crumbling, and people are misdirected. These aforementioned issues, come at the crux of a lack of education and mass incarceration. The roots are steeped in a system of inequality, that seeks to keep people enslaved.

Nelson Mandela declared, "Education is the most powerful weapon, which you can use to change the world." The power of education revolutionizes one's mind, which results in a radically revolutionized future. Education births knowledge of self, which unveils to you the purpose, gifts, and talents that God has implanted in your life.

Education is not an option anymore, it's a necessity more than ever before. These days, prisons are being built, based on elementary reading scores. There is a direct connection, between illiteracy and incarceration. We must provide avenues for our youth, to excel in colleges and universities, instead of being confined to prison cells.

Formal education will push you presently, but self-education will forge you into the future. The power of education, shuts the door on the past and grants you keys of knowledge, to unlock the door to your future. You have the power to change your future, but it begins with a changed mindset.

INCARCERATION NATION

America has a fascination, with mass incarceration. The United States has the largest prison population, in the world.

It also has the second highest rate, of incarceration per capita. We are incarceration nation. Our Black and Hispanic brothers, are incarcerated at a disproportionate rate, during their most productive years (18-38). Black males are incarcerated at 10 times, the rate of their White counterparts. To further assert, according to *The Atlantic* "one of every four Black men, born since the late 1970s, has spent time in prison, at profound cost to his family."

A number of the young brothers that I mentor, have a father who is incarcerated. Many of us have an incarcerated family member, friend, or have lost a loved one to an act of violence. Statistics suggest, 1 in 9 Black males, have a father in jail and 73 percent of Black men in jail, have no relationship with their father.

The mass incarceration of Black males, is simply neo-slavery or slavery by another name. We can't hide the fact that mass incarceration, is America's new slave plantation.

FREEDOM READERS

Published in 1845, *The Narrative of the Life of Frederick Douglass* contains a passage, "Once you learn to read, you will forever be free." According to the U.S. Census, there has been a continued decline and lack of interest, by young Black men toward books/literacy. As expressed by Dr. Kunjufu, "Time and time again when teachers say, open to page 34 in your textbooks, young boys close their minds and even close their eyes." We must use books that open the minds of our brothers, to build their character and foster a connectivity to literacy.

MEDIA AND THE MIND

Sadly, the minds of young men are enraptured by negative media perceptions. Oftentimes, the minds of our brothers, become shackled and chained by the crippling manacles, of ignorance on television. The continual perpetuation of fatherless homes, low self-esteem, drug culture, violence, and many other societal maladies are in need of remedies. The destiny of our brothers is not simply tied to sports and entertainment, but it's immersed in self-education and community empowerment. After all, Malcolm X did say, "Education is the passport to the future, for tomorrow belongs to those who prepare for it today."

We must build our brothers to rise from the ashes, like a phoenix, and overcome the odds. We must build them to breakthrough, with the intangibles for success, via the roads and routes of literacy. Essentially, after young men put the book down, we need to have opportunities for them to pick up.

BUILD PEOPLE, NOT PRISONS

There is a lack of reading proficiency that plays a critical role, in the lives of African American males who are imprisoned, in juvenile detention centers, victims, and perpetrators of gang violence, crime, etc. Mass incarceration has provided a pipeline, to ensure that our brothers remain illiterate and are imprisoned at length, for non-violent drug offenses.

During the years of 1993-2001, our nation was enamored by a cool politician, who had "southern swag." He even wore sunglasses and played the saxophone. Little did we know, that former President Bill Clinton, would become a pied piper for the policies that sent Black males to jail in record numbers. In 1994, Clinton signed into law the *Violent Crime Control Act*. It is the largest crime bill in the history of the United States, which provided $9.7 billion in funding for prisons.

The undercurrent language, to "clean up our streets" and "rid ourselves of crime" has always been to target Blacks. From Ronald Reagan's pseudo *War on Drugs*, to Bill Clinton's *Violent Crime Control Act*. These punitive measures have imposed tougher prison sentences, provided money for more prisons, and led to the mass incarceration of Black males. We have been maligned, oppressed, and victimized under the leadership of Republicans and Democrats in this nation. We must develop substantive communal and educational programs, that build people instead of prisons.

CRISIS IN COMMUNITIES

Exposing young men to rich literature, that relates to their lives, can begin to serve as a method to the madness. In the city of Detroit, we are facing challenges in education, that affect our communities. This paradigm ultimately impacts our schools, local economy, and overall environment. We need solutions, when approximately 1 in 3 Black and Hispanic males, in Detroit, does not graduate from high school.

According to the National Institute for Literacy, 47

percent of residents in the city of Detroit are "functionally illiterate." The meaning of functional illiteracy demarcates difficulties with reading, speaking, writing, and computational skills. This translates to roughly 200,000 people in the city, who read below a sixth grade reading level.

To further assert, the average Black 17-year-old reads at the proficiency level, of the average White 13-year-old. A four year difference in effective reading skills, provides a stark contrast. How do we close the Black and White achievement gap, to push our brothers to promising futures?

We must find proactive ways to engage African American males, in the reading experience. Detroit is a microcosm of the issues, that our brothers are facing in classrooms and communities, across America.

The overall achievement gap between African

American and White males, at the high school level is continually increasing. Many ninth grade Black males, are reading below grade level because of home factors, lack of relevant curriculum, low teacher expectations, and crippling societal factors.

These aforementioned factors are a problem, in relation to the progression of one's literacy acquisition. It is the foundation of being able to reason and communicate one's thoughts/feelings productively. When you can't express and verbalize your thoughts, oftentimes people will resort to negative ways to communicate their rage.

FINDING ANSWERS TO QUESTIONS

There are impending questions, that must be considered, in order to discover answers:

1. What factors cause Black males, to read below grade level?

2. How can educators make reading relevant, to young Black males?

3. What strategies can be used to increase reading productivity, in the lives of Black males?

PRE-HISTORIC PAGES?

The prospects of our brothers becoming successful in a technology driven age, without education, is slim to none. Reading is an essential building block, for African American males. Literacy is a fundamental framework for education, job security, and family life.

We are living in an age, where people would rather scroll through pictures on social media and watch videos online, than flip the pages on a book. Are books the new dinosaurs? In a technology age, have the pages of books, become archaic and pre-historic? How do we convey the power of reading material, to a techno-driven generation? I believe, it must be relatable and it must be relevant.

It's inherently wrong, when our schools fail to tap into the substance and skill set of our students. Something is wrong, when the same young male who fails Math and Economics, can go out in the street convert kilos to grams and grams to money. He is in a precarious position making money on the street, but failing math in school. His positive skills that weren't applied in the seats, are being used negatively in the streets.

MAKING READING RELEVANT

Alfred Tatum in his book, *Teaching Reading to Black Adolescent Males,* detailed that African American males often encounter barriers, that prevent them from academic achievement. The struggle of self-identity and self-concept, affect the way many young males behave. The spectrum of acting tough, gangs, violence, lack of self-disclosure, and disinterest in school often leads to suspension and even expulsion.

There is a glaring disconnect, between culturally relevant literature and classroom textbooks. This further places a gulf between the school and "struggling students." Much of the curriculum driven literature fails to connect to the culture and background of its students, causing a literacy disconnect to take place. Oftentimes, the literacy instruction does not meet the needs of African American adolescent males. Our Black boys need to see a reflection of themselves, in the books that they read. It helps to reaffirm, the purpose for reading.

Tatum noted that for the last 30 years, our schools have provided "disabling" texts to African American males, causing a gaping literacy disconnect. Reading content that reflects the culture of a student enables the reader. If the content is lacking cultural themes that resonate in the life of the student, that content is disabling.

These disabling texts, solely focus on skill and strategy development yet ignore the need to cultivate one's self-esteem, character, and personality. This is largely because policy decisions, are geared to measure one's reading output level versus content connectivity.

BRIDGES FOR OUR BROTHERS

As educators, mentors, and community innovators, we must fight to secure the educational standing of our brothers. This fight is also for the security of their livelihood, as productive citizens in America. If it is not protected, they will ultimately fall through the cracks. We must work to negate the narrative, of our brothers falling victim to the streets and/or the prison system. The true success story is in creating opportunities for our brothers, who live in the suburbs or come from tough streets.

We must create ways to captivate the minds of our

brothers, via the vehicle of relevant and rich literature. We must build positive relationships with our brothers via mentoring, discussions, and providing opportunities which will bring about change in their lives.

More than ever before, it is apparent that educators must captivate the minds of young boys. Sometimes the literature must be as bold and brash, as the music played in their headphones.

In the scholarly articles, *Bridges to Literacy for Boys* and *Saving Black Boys,* it's indicated that reading material must be relevant, surrounded by solutions that provide encouragement and hope. It is our job as educators, to build strong relationships with our students. We must learn who they are and provide relevant reading material, conducive to the climate and culture of the students, who we engage with on a daily basis.

All across the board, American boys are in crisis on

every academic level. Although education is at a crossroads, this is still the greatest time to create new opportunities, meet challenges and revolutionize the gamut of academia.

Psychologist Michael Thompson, was noted in Newsweek Magazine stating, "Girl behavior has become the gold standard and boys are treated, like defective girls."

A large number of boys, are being identified as learning disabled, emotionally unstable, and are suspended from school at an alarming rate. Why is it taking so long for people to realize, that much of what is happening in schools is not working?

According to the U.S. Department of Justice, "24 percent of girls have been suspended from school at least once by age 17, but so have 42 percent of boys." The Manhattan Institute found that "65 percent of boys who start high school, graduate four years later, compared with 72 percent of girls."

The University of Michigan study found that "62 percent of female high school seniors, plan to graduate from a four-year-college, compared with 51 percent of male students." These facts spotlight the issues, that boys are facing in the classroom, college, and ultimately in the community.

FACTS VS. TRUTH

The sad reality, is that prison has now become a rites of passage for our boys, primarily African American males. How did this happen? It happened under our watch, as we sought to live a better life, but not build better lives for our brothers in the community.

According to researchers, "60 percent of the incarcerated juveniles under 18 years of age, were African American and mostly male." Without a doubt, there is an increasing overrepresentation of Black youth and men in jails. There is a stark interconnection, between education and mass incarceration. This is not just a physical prison, but oftentimes a prison without bars, ultimately locking people out of access and opportunity

We can reverse the curse. In chapter four, I mentioned that 85 percent of all juvenile offenders rate, as functionally or marginally illiterate. If we teach our brothers to read and provide them with adequate skills to succeed, they would have an 85 percent chance of NOT being a juvenile offender or going to jail. We can reverse the negative trajectory.

We must inform our brothers, about life's bitter truths and harsh realities. The choices are narrowing, it's either education or incarceration. Advocates, mentors, parents, and teachers must inform our boys about the opportunities that education provides and help them to overcome life's hurdles.

Many of our Black boys are being pushed into prison, rather than Princeton. Society has created avenues for jail, rather than Cornel and Yale. The system would rather see our brothers, serve four years in a state pen, instead of four years at Penn State.

Research has provided evidence, that Black boys have disproportionately high numbers, among those who are struggling readers. Every parent, teacher, and school leader must demand that Black boys experience reading success by third grade and beyond, simply because jails are full of our brothers who cannot read. Communities are void of formidable opportunities, for residents who are illiterate.

According to the National Association of Educational Progress, "69 percent of African American children cannot read at grade level in the fourth grade, compared with 29 percent among White children."

Despite the disconcerting facts, the truth is we must hold schools, communities, government entities, and ourselves accountable to see to it that our brothers and sisters, receive a proper education. If they don't, we know that the spectrum of incarceration looms greatly. It's an injustice, when prisons are in better conditions than schools and neighborhoods. It's an injustice, when a child lives in an impoverished community and receives a poor education. It's an injustice, when schools lack the adequate amenities, to prepare youth to compete in a global economy.

How can a child be motivated to walk to school, when they have to watch their back because of an unsafe environment? How can you walk to school confidently, when your city refuses to install street lights? The basic necessities must be met, for our people to make adequate progress.

TALKING WHITE OR TALKING RIGHT?

Far too many times, academic achievement in our community, is viewed as "selling out." This indictment has made it plausible, to praise lack and shun achievement. Too many people will praise a sports star, quicker than celebrate a child's A's and B's, on their report card.

A brother who enunciates and pronounces his words, is often considered as "talking White." If being smart is "acting White" than what is "acting Black?" Since when did being Black, become a standard for ignorance? We must eradicate a fragmented failure mentality.

What message does this send to our brothers, with its connection to valuing education? Does this make our brothers, shy away from being smart? How do we make being smart, the new cool? We must create a value system surrounding education, rather than minimize its outlook.

We can't dismiss academic achievement as something that's "soft, White, or feminine." We come from a resilient people who fought for the right to be educated, choosing rather to die so we might reap the benefits.

We don't celebrate academics, like we celebrate athletic achievements. We show more love to the brother who made it to the NBA, than we do to the brother who earned an MBA. Our brothers are bright enough, to analyze our value system. As a result, they choose what brings them the most praise. We must praise brothers who chose books over the block, school over the streets, and encourage them to come back and improve their communities.

To choose school and higher education, is even more difficult, when the odds are stacked against you. We praise the streets but not the scholars. We throw a party for the brother who got out of jail, but barely pat the brother on the back, who graduated from college.

Many of our brothers, are targets of the judicial system and we must create avenues of opportunity, to reduce recidivism. We must quell animosity and make the education of our people are priority. The real "sell out" is the one who refuses to speak truth to power. The "sell out" is the one, who pushes dope, rather than hope to our people. We must give back, use our talents, and give of ourselves to enrich the people in our communities.

THE SKIN I'M IN

We live in a culture, that privileges Whites and grants access to Black people with European features. We appropriate that in our culture and celebrate those with "good hair, lighter skin, thinner noses, and smaller lips." The summation is that those individuals are more aesthetically appealing. This perception is indicative of the sick pathology, of cultural racism, due to White supremacy.

Dr. Michael Eric Dyson, poetically proclaimed, "Being light, bright, and almost white may be beautiful to many. However, being dark in the park, like bark is a beautiful thing as well." We often put ourselves down, if we don't possess Eurocentric features.

Who said your hair was nappy or kinky? The only naps and kinks, are the ones in your mind. I've got good hair, because I've got African in my family. Who said your lips were too big? Open your mouth and speak words of love, to yourself and your people. Speak truth to power, against systemic racism. Who said your nose was too big? You're alive to breathe the pristine air, that sustains your life. You're not too dark or too light, God made you just right! Raise your self-esteem, look in the mirror, and affirm yourself. Your skin is not a curse. Love the skin you're in!

As a brown skin brother, I personally struggled with a complex growing up as a kid. For many years, I did not feel comfortable in my own skin. I didn't always feel that "Black is beautiful." I couldn't always say it loud, like James Brown, "I'm Black and I'm proud." I didn't always love the skin, that I'm in. Of course that led to depression, insecurity, and feelings of inadequacy. All of which, I had to overcome and heal from.

My mother and brother, are both light skin. At times, I literally felt like the "black sheep" of the family. My father is my complexion, but he wasn't in the home to affirm me. As a result, I saw how I was treated differently, even by my own people. At a very young age, I realized that I didn't have the "skin to win." In the media, I would see men and women, who were the same complexion as me (or darker) facing greater hurdles. They were marginalized, criminalized, and rarely regarded as being attractive.

When I began to gain a greater appreciation for

myself, see my value, and recognize my worth then I began to love the skin that I am in. I had to come to the realization that being Black is not a curse, in fact it's a blessing. As I studied my history, I began to love myself and the people who look like me. I began to operate out of self-love, rather than self-hate. If you don't love yourself, you can't truly love anybody else. Especially those who look like you.

We have to start seeing our greatness through our lens, not through the cultural cataracts of White supremacy and European inferiority. The complexity and double consciousness of African Americans, is in direct proximity to the culture that makes them a prisoner in their own skin. The senseless, light skin versus dark skin feud is just another tactic used, to keep Black people from being unified. It was rooted in slavery and continues, to be an indictment to our own community. The more melanin that our brothers and sisters have, the more menacing they are portrayed to be in the media.

URBAN RENEWAL OR URBAN UPHEAVAL?

While we're arguing with each other, over varying degrees of skin complexion, redlining and repositioning is taking place in our face. Urban demographic repositioning is happening in our communities. We are in an onslaught against the reformation of gentrification, as Black people are being systematically removed from urban spaces. James Baldwin asserted that "Urban renewal, means Negro removal." We are seeing those prophetic words, unveil before our eyes today.

EDUCATION AND HIP-HOP

Much of rap and hip-hop music is maligned, for it's bombastic lyrical content. The focus of education and hip-hop is rarely, if ever, lifted to a state of academic analysis. Due to mass media influences, much of it's conscious messaging has been diluted. In its innovative infancy, hip-hop was the community's *CNN Headline News* of its day.

The rhetorical genius, Tupac Shakur used prolific prose, to rap about a rose that grew through concrete. Although his art and reality blurred the lines, we could see glimmers of greatness, through the lens of his life. He poured his soul into songs like *Brenda's Got A Baby*, *Keep Ya Head Up*, *Dear Mama*, and the list goes on.

Many fail to realize that Tupac read incessantly, merging the arts and literature. He is the son of Black Panther, Afeni Shakur. Tupac was born a month, after his mother was acquitted of more than 150 charges of, conspiracy against the United States government. In his early years, Tupac attended the Baltimore School for the Arts. He studied acting, poetry, jazz, and even ballet.

His life was mired, in painful "poetic injustice" yet he masterfully merged literacy and the arts together.

We always talk about the rappers who claim, to have sold drugs or have a particular beef with a rival rapper. We celebrate "the college dropout" but not the college graduate. The skewed objectification and media perception, rarely sheds light on the rappers who attain education. The following is a list of artists, who are lyrically equipped and educationally empowered:

- David Banner attended Southern University in Louisiana, where he majored in Business Administration. He later earned a Masters Degree in Education, from the University of Maryland.

- Ludacris studied Music Management and graduated in the top five percent of his class, from Georgia State University.

- Talib Kweli studied Experimental Theater at New York University.

- Flavor Flav, of Public Enemy, is a self-taught pianist who attended Adelphi University in New York, along with Chuck D.

- An uncommon rapper, named Common attended Florida A&M University. He studied Business Administration.

- The metaphorical rapper, Lil Wayne, was in the gifted and talented program as a high school honor student. He attended the University of Houston, majoring in Political Science and the University of Phoenix for Psychology.

- Ice Cube studied Architectural Drafting, at the Phoenix Institute of Technology.

- The rapper Plies, attended Miami University and the University of Central Florida for Nursing.

- J. Cole attended St. John's University in New York City on an academic scholarship. He majored in Communications and minored in Business, graduating magna cum laude.

- 2 Chainz attended Alabama State University, after finishing second best in his high school class. He later attended Virginia State University, graduating with honors.

- Ryan Leslie at the age of 14, scored a 1600 on his SATs. He graduated from Harvard at the age of 19, with a degree in Government and Macroeconomics.

Brother, if you want to be a rapper, you need to also be a reader. How can you rap about, what you don't have the vocabulary to express? Balance the lyrical bars and the literary books. It's okay to have a Bachelor's degree and a brash delivery!

LIFE AND DEATH

The well-being of our brothers, hangs in the balance in a country that has all of the amenities, to secure opportunities for them, yet willingly turns a blind eye to their needs. Colin Powell declared, "The education of our children is a matter of life and death. If our Black boys cannot read, then jails are waiting for them. If our Black boys cannot read, then opportunities for employment will not be available to them. If our Black boys cannot read, they will not be able to participate in civil discourse. If our Black boys cannot read, then when they become parents, they will not teach their children how to read and the cycle of struggle will continue."

We have to break the cycle, of illiteracy and incarceration. This predicament is directly connected, to the generations of tomorrow. There is a glaring overrepresentation of Black boys in special education, throughout America's school system. Black boys are three times more likely, than Whites to be in special education. The suspension and expulsion rate for Black boys, is three times the rate for any other student. These disproportionate rates, are a mirror image of the impacts on Black lives in the judicial system. Many cities throughout the United States, have less than 30 percent, of Black boys graduating from high school.

NATIONAL EPIDEMIC

The Schott Foundation, which collects data on Black boys throughout the United States, further explains the educational epidemic affecting Black boys:

Expulsions and suspensions:
Black boys make up only 8.6 percent of public school enrollments, yet they represent 22 percent of students expelled from school and 23 percent of students suspended.

Dropouts:
Overall 25 percent - 30 percent of America's teenagers fail
to graduate from high school. However, that figure soars to
an astounding rate, for 50 percent of Black male students in
the United States.

Special Education:
Black students nationwide are 2.9 times, as likely as Whites,
to be designated as mentally challenged. They are also 1.9
times as likely, to be designated as having an emotional
problem. They are 1.3 times as likely, to be labeled as
having a learning disability. Research suggests that 80
percent of children in special education, are there because of
a reading deficiency. Overall twice as many Black boys, are
in special education programs than Black girls.

Graduation:
Only 50 percent of Black males earn high school diplomas,
compared to 80 percent of White males and 86 percent of
White females.

Juvenile Incarceration:
Black males under the age of 18, are three times more likely,
to be incarcerated than White males.

Unemployment:
Close to 25 percent of Black youth ages 16 to 19, were not
employed nor in school. This statistic is twice the national
average and six times the national rate, for unemployment.

SELF-CONCEPT

The aforementioned statistics, serve as a wake up call. We

can't continue to do business as usual. Amidst the alarming statistics, we must empower our brothers to be standouts against all odds. Schools should provide content rich texts, which move beyond a sole focus on skill and strategy development to include a social, cultural, and economic focus.

Alfred Tatum suggested, "Many boys experience school as an assault on their identities and on their masculinity. They believe that their existence simply doesn't matter. Disproportionately referred for disciplinary actions and assigned to special education placements, they see little reason to navigate this path of humiliation. Many end up dropping out of school, which is largely because policy decisions are geared to measure one's reading output level versus their reasoning."

I AM...MY BROTHER'S KEEPER!

CHAPTER 6

Raising and Teaching Boys

A frican American males often encounter barriers, that prevent them from academic achievement. These academic barriers, become precursors for prison bars. Alfred Tatum notes, "It is often difficult, for many Black boys to make it through the four critical years, after middle school and before college." He calls these years, "The Black male's Bermuda Triangle." Tatum suggests, "Many young Black males, who make it through middle and high school, attribute their success to personal motivation and self-determination."

Literacy instruction is an avenue, that nurtures the qualities of motivation and character development. To accomplish this, teachers need to select texts and plan activities, that will foster the development of our students' cultural, social, and emotional literacies. The success of our brothers without adequate literacy development, is greatly diminished.

Every mentoring organization must incorporate some level of literacy development. Mentoring has to place reading, as a focal point in the development of our brothers.

IDENTITY AND MASCULINITY

The struggles of self-identity and self-concept, affect the way many young males behave. The cycle of acting tough, gangs, violence, lack of self-disclosure, and disinterest in school are attributed to this identity crisis. It's often a false bravado, that our young men perpetuate to mask the vulnerability behind it. Many of the negative behaviors lead to suspensions and even expulsions. These behaviors add to the negative stereotypes, that are ingrained in the minds of teachers.

Many of our brothers are from low socioeconomic communities and high-risk neighborhoods. Oftentimes, instructors fail to understand the ramifications. As a result, there is a lack of focus in school due to students being consumed with concerns, about their safety and struggles in their homes/neighborhoods.

BATTLE OF THE SEXES

No one can avoid the issue of gender in the classroom, some would convey, "it's the elephant in the room." According to Leonard Sax, "The gender issue is relevant to classroom learning in more ways than one. Increasingly, young boys are saying that "school is stupid." They continue to express, a disdain for reading. This growing response cuts across all demographic groups, affecting affluent White boys in the suburbs and Black boys in urban communities.

The issue of reading and disdain for books, has become a growing epidemic amongst boys in America. As aforementioned, the gender issue regarding books is no respecter of persons or socioeconomic status. Sax noted an interview with a young boy, who expressed a great dislike for books, declaring "I'd rather be burned at the stake, than read a book." It was also noted, that the boy is a child of college educated parents. Assuming that a child of academic achievers, would automatically fall in love with books, is quite the contrary.

According to Sax, "The gender gap did not widen because girls are reading more; they're not. In fact, girls are slightly less likely to read in their spare time today." He expressed that 9 out of 10 boys, have stopped reading altogether. What kinds of books have 90 percent of boys read, to find no value in reading altogether? The idea of being a reader and being a boy/man are not incompatible. Rich books that relate to our brothers, help to affirm their masculinity rather than diminish it.

FOUR FACTORS

According to researchers, there are four distinct factors that push boys away from books:

1. Changes in education over the past three decades.

2. Increased dependence on technology and video games.

3. Medications for ADD (Attention Deficit Disorder) and ADHD (Attention Deficit Hyperactivity Disorder).

4. Devaluation of masculinity.

We cannot ignore these factors. We must analyze them, by using the paradigm shifts in education and technology, to develop a generation of literacy learners. Educators, parents, and mentors must find engaging ways to foster literacy development, within the minds of our boys via rich literature and cutting edge content.

REACH TO TEACH

Teachers often tell me, "It's hard teaching this particular student (mainly boys). He won't listen. He won't cooperate. He won't do anything." These conversations take place during teacher meetings and in staff lounges, each day in America.

I generally discover, that there is no positive relational engagement, between the student and teacher. You can say "sit down and be quiet" all day, until you're blue in the face. Nothing will change, until your approach changes. It's easy to neglect someone, that you only see as an object. Things will change in our homes, communities, and classrooms when we change our words from "these kids" to "our kids." You can't inspire and instruct our kids, if you refuse to identify with our kids. Essentially, something that you deem to be yours, you treat differently. If it belongs to you, then you treat it with TLC. Our children are no different and they need "Tender Loving Care." Oftentimes, the harder the exterior, the more love that is needed on the interior. We have to provide it!

The issues intensify, when teachers are responsible for instructing Black boys. How can I relate to someone of a different gender, from a different generation, and who is of a different race? Begin to search for similarities, rather than glaring differences.

We must think critically and metacognitively. How do we engage a generation, that would rather pick up their phone to text, than pick up a book to read text? How do we engage a generation, that would rather be entertained than informed? Oftentimes, our young people are more interested, in Beyonce than biology. They know more about

Dr. Dre, than they do about Dr. King. How do we engage a generation, that is more focused on athletics than academics? How do we appeal to those, who are more familiar with hurt and hate, than they are with love?

We must have 3D vision, through Dignity and Diversity, in order to unlock the Dreams of our brothers and sisters. The power of engagement, must also be ascertained, through relationships, rigor, and relevance.

You can never instruct, who you are afraid of. When you approach students in love, that automatically eliminates fear. If you don't believe particular students can succeed, you will never equip them with the intangibles to be successful. An apathetic attitude and approach, coupled with timidity will negate every opportunity, to reach people in any setting. The saying goes, "People don't care how much you know, until they know how much you care." You can't engage in successful rearing and teaching, without first reaching them. Our brothers can tell, if you really care for them and are committed to their well-being.

BOYS AND BOOKS

Illiteracy underscores the inability, to read or write fluently. Juxtaposed with *illiteracy* is the term, *aliteracy*. The spectrum of *aliteracy,* is the state of being able to read but being uninterested in doing so. The most illiterate person, is not the one who can't read. It's the one who can, but won't read. Mark Twain declared, "A person who won't read, has no advantage over one who can't read."

In a digital age, we are seeing an increasing number of people dependent on technology. The preference of choice has become to use your phone and text, rather than open a book to read text. Many boys are lacking social engagement and mental stimulation, via the books provided in the classroom. There is an impending disconnect, between the reading that is brought into the classroom and the relevance of it to boys.

Many boys are uninterested and disconnected from the building blocks of reading. Boys who seem uninterested in literacy in the classroom, may very well be enthusiastic readers and writers in different contexts. However, they will never discover it, if they are not exposed to it. The rigidity of literacy practices that appeal to boys, are rarely valued in the context of institutionalized school literacy. The particular appeal or genre that boys express interest, is often overlooked, to the frustration of both student and teacher in the classroom setting.

Many schools frown upon boys reading books, that contain violence. Researchers have indicated, that for boys, the reading genres that are preferred are connected to action, violence, and popular culture. All of which are normally prohibited in the classroom. Teachers who encourage student choice, via reading and writing, on a variety of subject spectrums, can channel the literacy practices of boys.

Our boys often use literacy practices when they visit websites about sports, video games, discuss the plot of movies and television programs. Most instructors and parents, give no adaptive cognitive energy to it. Simply because it is outside the parameters, of the ways we have been trained to learn. Many times we are oblivious to the obvious. The same energy that our brothers use to run and play, must be used to learn academically. If you lift weights then you will gain muscles. If you lift a book to read, then you will gain mental strength.

William Brozo affirms, "Teachers should rely on more discovery than scholarship, in their adaptation to the reading development of boys." The opportunity for reading choice and exposure to varied genres, is highly suggested. Schools must reveal to our boys, their significance and the books we use must be significant. There must be allotted time in our schools, to tap into personal interests and passions, as it relates to reading. In addition, he found through interviews with teachers, that boys that were given the opportunity to read materials that aligned with their interests, "led to encounters with texts that heightened reading engagement and their achievement in language arts."

Brozo stated, "We must infuse powerful literature into the minds of boys, that meet them at their interest level and lifts them to a higher cognitive plane." For instance, in one of his interviews, a teacher used the lyrics to a few popular songs of the boys in his class to study vocabulary, decoding, sounds, and syllables. The vocabulary and comprehension test scores of these boys improved dramatically. Brozo affirmed that examples such as this, creates a bridge between student competencies, with familiar texts and their classroom experiences. This increases student engagement in learning and expands, the literacy abilities of male readers.

CLOSING THE GAP

There is a disconnect between the literature in the textbook or prescribed reading material, that places a gulf between the school and the struggling student. Oftentimes, literacy instruction does not meet the needs, of African American adolescent males.

Tatum suggests that we must reshape the trajectory of reading. He notes that "must-read texts" should have four characteristics:

1. Must be intellectually exciting for both students and teachers.

2. Serve as a roadmap and provide apprenticeship.

3. Challenge students to think critically and cognitively.

4. Help students apply literacy skills and strategies independently.

Teachers must select appropriate reading materials, in order to engage African American adolescent males with text. Reading material must provide a rich literature experience, that is culturally competent, to the needs of adolescent males.

Tatum suggests, "A meaningful literacy program, should include texts that shape a positive life trajectory and provide a roadmap, that can help students resist non-productive behaviors." Rich literacy experiences address the needs of students academically, culturally, emotionally, and socially. A literacy program should include texts that provide solutions to problems and strategies to be successful.

VIOLENCE AND BOOKS

We have heard time and time again, about the connection

between entertainment (music, movies, video games) and violence. The assertion is that the aforementioned genres, impact people to commit crimes. The ambiguity of research, has led many to indicate that other factors become contributors, to one's aggression and violence.

What songs or movies, make you want to hurt somebody? Of course your mother or grandmother, would not approve of many song lyrics or movies. However, you listened to the song, because you liked the melody and/or the artist. You watched the movie, because you were intrigued and/or it was entertaining. What makes our boys any different?

Do books with violent topics and plots, influence boys to partake in aggressive/violent behavior? Many teachers become frustrated, when boys read and write about material deemed to be of a violent nature.

Oftentimes, the the types of literacy practices to

which boys are often influenced by, are connected to action, violence, and popular culture, which are usually prohibited in the classroom. In the classroom, the emphasis is often placed on high-culture literature, driven by character development.

Schools have assumed that banning violent books and writing, will offset the desire for boys to engage in violent behavior. Generally, this is not the case. Putting on your superman or superwoman cape, to snatch a "violent" book out of someone's hand will only increase their curiosity. What are you attempting to save them from? Educators are often misguided by that belief and rather than bring it into the classroom to address, teachers make the mistake of shunning it.

B.T. Williams suggests, "Violent reading and writing brings with it the fear that such violence might erupt beyond the page into the classroom." Contrary to that belief, boys are not solely drawn to stories of blood, gore, horror, and the trappings of crime/violence. In fact it is the suspense, not the violence, that compels boys to delve into a specific genre.

In actuality, many of the books that have violent undertones, address the harsh realities of the world and are often broached with today's issues, decision making, friendship bonds, and interconnectedness. Williams notes, "The underlying fear, is that boys cannot distinguish between the violence in a story and the violence in real life, or that they are unable to process imaginative work, but instead absorb it and are molded by it without thinking." This is why powerful discussions with boys is important, in order to bridge the disconnect. We should also give more consideration and credit, to the logical thinking skills and decision making, that boys inherently possess.

CRITICAL CROSSROADS

We are at a critical and crucial crossroads in education. The education of our Black boys must not be taken lightly, but it specifically has life or death ramifications. I find it disheartening, that our brothers can get guns and drugs, that will destroy them, quicker than they can get access to books that will empower them. When the death grip of guns and drugs doesn't vanquish their life, it is the death grip of grasping the bars of a prison cell, that society has projected to be their fate.

Dr. Jawanza Kunjufu, noted that there is a direct link between illiteracy and imprisonment which impacts lives, families, and generations. The Schott Foundation's facts about Black boys, highlighted the increasing rates of Black youth in the criminal justice system, with 60 percent under the age of 18.

DISDAIN AND DISCONNECT

The texts that are often used in the classroom, continually fail to connect to the issues that our young boys are experiencing. The issues of self-identity and self-concept must be examined, so that our boys can truly define who they are and their purpose. Our classrooms need books that are culturally compatible, in order to enable our brother's thinking and connect beyond their world.

Peg Tyre wrote in Newsweek magazine that "Society treats boys, like defective girls." Our boys have stopped reading. Much of it is due to video games, changes in education, and the devaluation of masculinity. Educators must stimulate the minds of boys with books, that are relevant to their lives and use those books as a springboard to discuss issues.

Rich literature that provides connections, will speak to one's inner significance and personal value. Our boys must be able to open books and see themselves reflected, in the literature that they read. Many educators have demonized books, with violent themes, that many boys enjoy reading.

The belief that those books lead to violence, is simply not true. If our boys are reading these books, we as educators should be able to discuss the themes represented in the books regarding decision making, lifestyle, defining masculinity, and the present choices that impact one's future.

SURVEY SAYS

In the mentoring and literacy development of our brothers, via my program *Boys 2 Books*, I decided to conduct a case study. I randomly selected 15 boys. The students were ninth grade African American males. The boys were also residents of the Metro Detroit area.

A portion of the materials, included a reading survey

that I used for the study. The survey was used, according to a Likert scale. During my study, I juxtaposed qualitative and quantitative research results. The study investigated the reading habits of African-American males, in the ninth grade. The boys provided information, on how much time they spent reading, what they were reading, if they dislike reading, and their reading interests.

Upon the survey findings, I discovered a glaring disconnect. The reading survey, showed that 53 percent of the boys "never" read for 30 minutes or more daily. Yet, 53 percent "always" thought they were good readers. How can our boys expect to become better readers, if they aren't consistently engaged in the reading process? The lack of time spent reading, can affect one's level of language acquisition.

In my data collection, I used a particular question to guide my research. "What factors cause African American males, to read below grade level?" The substratum of the

aforementioned question, prompted two additional

questions:

1. How can educators, make reading relevant to African American males?

2. What strategies can be used, to increase reading productivity amongst African American males?

DATA DRIVEN

The data showed that 66 percent of the boys, "sometimes"

felt that reading was boring. The enjoyment of reading

aloud in class and visiting the library, was experienced

"sometimes" by 46 percent of the boys. The reading survey

results suggested that "sometimes" the boys like to read

and "sometimes" reading is boring to them. However, the

overarching majority of the young boys are not spending

much time reading.

As noted in many literature reviews, "A Black

male's chances for success, are diminished without literacy development." The data also showed that boredom and disdain for reading diminishes greatly, when boys make an independent selection of reading material. Providing opportunities for student selection and choice, is essential to their success.

The reading survey results suggested that 53 percent of the boys, "sometimes" read books for enjoyment. Teachers must select appropriate reading materials, in order to engage African American adolescent males with text.

The majority (53 percent) of boys prefer to choose their own books to read. When boys are provided opportunities, to read books that align with their interests, it strengthens their overall reading engagement. The data also showed, that the main reading genre of choice, were action books. For boys, the primary reading genres preferred are connected to action, sports, violence, and popular culture.

This study asserts, that reading is a central factor in the development of Black boys, helping them to avoid many of life's pitfalls. According to Kunjufu, "If our Black boys cannot read, then jails are waiting for them. If our Black boys cannot read, then opportunities for employment will not be available to them."

IMPORTANCE AND IMPACT

Thomas Newkirk poignantly stated, "Reading is so necessary for African American males, because it will serve as a fundamental building block for their education, job security, and family life." Reading is a fundamental building block, that impacts every part of the lives of our Black boys.

Educators and parents, must place powerful and rich literature into the hands of our boys that expand the parameters of their minds. Rich literature will take them places, beyond their environment and speak to the greatness, that often lies dormant in their lives.

The relationships, research, and results of my findings yielded an inside perspective, into the thoughts and attitudes of our brothers concerning reading. I have committed myself, to the work of empowering our brothers. I am committed to changing the negative narrative, that is perpetuated against our brothers. I desire to provide opportunities for success, help our brothers realize their purpose, and develop their love for reading. We must work to impact the lives of Black boys in profound ways, with books that speak to their character development, masculinity, overcoming obstacles, and life-long goals.

SINGLE PARENT STRUGGLES

To my single parent Mothers, I urge you, don't give up on

our sons. I'm the product of a single parent mother, who didn't give up on me! She refused to give up on me, even when I wanted to give up on myself. Her love, discipline, and commitment, propelled me to higher heights. Of course a two-parent household is preferred. Yet, one good parent, is better than two bad parents.

There were times when I was bitter and angry, because my father was absent in my life. I had to discover ways to channel that energy proactively, through sports, music, and writing. Later in life, I forgave my father and transformed being bitter to becoming better. You can't heal from the pain, if you don't deal with it. You will truly begin to live, when you forgive.

I chose to give young brothers, what I didn't receive from my father; mentorship, guidance, a listening ear, and commitment to their success.

Yes, I faced peer pressure and the lure of the streets.

However, it was my fight with cancer, that redirected my life. Without a praying mama, you wouldn't be reading these words today. Even when our brothers and sons are angry, much of it is displaced because as a single mother or mentor, you stand in proxy for an absentee father. Correct him, love him, but don't give up on him.

Researchers affirm, the average father, spends seven minutes a day with his children. The average mother, spends 34 minutes a day with her children. Between the two parents, is only 41 minutes of time, spent with their children. Who and what has our children's minds, for the other 23 hours? It's imperative that we spend more time, with our children.

There must be a return of strong fathers, in our homes and children's lives. You may be divorced, but don't divorce yourself from your children. Brother, just because you're not with her, doesn't grant license to abandon your children. Dear sister, don't use the children as punishment towards him by restricting his access. You are both parents and must find common ground, to place the needs of your children above your egos. Our brothers need to be present and have a presence, in the lives of our children.

FAMILY LITERACY

Family literacy is a key component, to fostering literacy acquisition amongst our brothers. According to Dr. Mary Bigler, "Children should learn, 70 new words per week and know at least 60,000 words by the end of twelfth grade." How will this take place, if our youth take no interest in reading at all?

You will be surprised by the number of young people, who don't have books in their homes. Oftentimes the attitude of youth toward reading, is shaped by parents/ family. I have grown increasingly concerned, about parents/

family attitudes towards reading and the impact it has on our boys.

What is the solution to the illiteracy malady? Literacy begins in the home. The National Center for Education reports that "Only 45 percent of parents, read to their children." Children who are read to, or read with their parents have greater phonemic awareness, comprehension, fluency, speech recognition, communicative, and verbal ability. Parental literacy is one of the major predictors, of a child's future success.

Many of the boys that I mentor, have expressed that they were never read to as a child. The power of pre-literacy exposure, is a key ingredient and indicator to unlocking the power of one's reading prowess. I encourage parents to read to their children. This shapes a child's language acquisition, phonemic awareness, comprehension, and vocabulary development.

A parent must become, the first teacher in their child's life. It's critical that parents begin to recognize their power, to demand and create change. Parents have to do more than attend sporting events, or buy outfits for prom and homecoming. It's incumbent to attend Parent Teacher Conferences and PTA meetings. Your presence is pertinent, to your child's performance.

The best way to teach our boys, is to reach them where they are. When you meet someone on their level, with an open ear to listen and learn, you can then begin to provide transformative information. We must be equipped with determination, in order to spark and stimulate the imagination, of our brothers in the classroom and community. They are indeed scholars and graduates, not inmates and delinquents.

According to the National Institute for Literacy, "Seven million people, cannot read words. In addition, 27 million, cannot read well enough, to fill out a job application." Overall 30 million Americans, cannot read a sentence. We must partner with local literacy organizations, to increase literacy in the community, and promote a greater level of reading development in the classroom.

We must protect our youth and ensure that their promised future, will be greater than the present plight they face. We must use our creative ingenuity, to develop innovative methods, to captivate the minds of our brothers. Powerful engagement, empowers them to find knowledge in books and a greater discovery of self.

I AM...MY BROTHER'S KEEPER!

CHAPTER 7

Ain't No Love in the Streets

I came across a quote that stated, "The streets will kidnap you, raise you, and then return you to your family so they can bury you." This is the unfortunate dilemma in our communities that are void of love, servant leaders, safety, and adequate access to opportunities.

The infrastructure to incubate a cesspool of negativity, was designed to decimate our communities. Structural and societal racism has constructed barriers, to thwart our progression and upward mobility. It continues to work, when there is rampant division in our communities.

MISSION MINDED

So many times we are heavenly minded, that we remain no earthly good. We must be mission minded, beyond our places of worship. It's a sad indictment if the messages we preach and convey, ultimately outshine the lives we live. The best sermon given, is not solely what is said during the service, but rather how you live after the service. Our service should be exemplified with our life, not just by our lips. Our service should spill out into our communities, to bring hope and healing to the lives of others.

MATTHEW 25 ALIVE

In a familiar passage of scripture, Matthew 25:35-40, we find Jesus declaring these words:

35 For I was an hungred, and ye gave me meat: I was thirsty, and ye gave me drink: I was a stranger, and ye took me in:

36 Naked, and ye clothed me: I was sick, and ye visited me: I was in prison, and ye came unto me.

165

37 Then shall the righteous answer him, saying, Lord, when saw we thee an hungred, and fed thee? or thirsty, and gave thee drink?

38 When saw we thee a stranger, and took thee in? or naked, and clothed thee?

39 Or when saw we thee sick, or in prison, and came unto thee?

40 And the King shall answer and say unto them, Verily I say unto you, Inasmuch as ye have done it unto one of the least of these my brethren, ye have done it unto me.

What is the responsibility, of the religious community and the church? For so long, the church has been the epicenter of the Black community and it now seems to have lost its prophetic voice. Have we lost our fervor for the least, the lost, the left out, and the overlooked? We have to make Matthew 25, come alive in each day in the lives of our brothers and sisters. It goes beyond religious affiliation and brings about reconciliation, to invoke the fact that your life matters.

We must address and remedy the ever-existing needs

of our people, whose voices aren't heard and who are rarely provided a seat at the table. This is the engine that forges us together, to build the beloved community.

The responsibility of the church, far extends beyond buying cars and jets, to keeping our communities safe, our brothers off the streets and of jails. Our responsibility, has to exceed the doors of our homes and places of worship. If not then those same issues, that we are trying to avoid will pry open the doors of our homes and places of worship.

What is the responsibility of the church, in regards to education, from the pastor on the pulpit, to members in the pew? Our churches must offer academic enrichment programs, year round, even if the government does not fund them. Yes, we learn about Jesus on Sunday, but many of our brothers lack the skills, to read about him Monday through Saturday. We are adequately prepared to get to Heaven, but inadequately prepared to deal with the hell that our people are facing. We're having church, praying, singing songs, and shouting but our brothers are dying in the streets. We need to go in the streets and pray, sing, and shout. We need to go in the streets and feed our brothers and sisters. Our prayers are ricocheting off the walls in our church, only to bring results in the lives of its congregants.

There is a generation of young people, who know hip-hop but not hymns. They know Jay-Z and Jeezy, but not Jesus. They know how to fight, but they don't know spiritual warfare. They know how to cuss, but they don't know how to pray. They don't have "church attire" but they have a desire to be better. Will we embrace this generation and love them or shun them?

Yes, there are churches doing the work of ministry beyond their walls. However, more of us must work together to catapult our communities. We are not individually isolated, rather we must be collectively connected.

CATCHING HELL

Where do our brothers go, when recreation centers are closed, apprenticeships are scarce, employment opportunities are slim to none (even with education), and schools are closed yet prisons are open? We are seen as a pariah and persona non grata, of the larger culture and enemy amongst our own people. We expect racism externally, but the intra-racial racism that we exact on ourselves internally, has dealt a severe blow to our community.

They always say, "How do we fix and save the Black male? He is an endangered species." They never ask, "How can we build stronger Black males?" They approach us from a deficit, not as an asset. As a result, our communities have been socially engineered to engender a deficit model. We are seeing too many of our people, striving to survive, yet void of the resources to thrive.

The structure of racism has caused our displaced anger, to be pillaged upon each other and turn on those who look like us. You can't say, "I am *My Brother's Keeper*" while being a predator and destroyer, of your brothers at the same time. How can you say that you love God that you have never seen, but hate your brother who you see everyday?

There is an impending disconnect, that we have not yet bridged. Essentially, how can you lift your hands to God, but won't stretch your hands to help your brother? In fact, you become a hypocrite and a liar.

How can we holler on Sunday and then remain quiet, as we watch our brothers and sisters catch hell, Monday through Saturday? We cannot continue to stick our heads in the sand and expect problems to go away. We must recognize our true power, collectively and internally. We must not turn away from issues, we must be bold enough to address them head on.

NEW MOVEMENT

In his final speech, "I've Been To The Mountaintop" The Rev. Dr. Martin Luther King, Jr. declared, "It's alright to talk about the New Jerusalem, but one day, you must talk about the new New York, the new Atlanta, the new Philadelphia, the new Los Angeles, the new Memphis, Tennessee. This is what we have to do."

We have enough monuments, we have plenty of community events, but we need a mission minded movement. A movement that goes beyond ego, but is bold enough to empower all of us to grow. We have to strategize, mobilize, and organize it. We must turn the rhetoric into reconciliation and responsibility. In so doing, we can create a new narrative, sharing our stories of strength as assets and advocates.

CHANGING THE NARRATIVE

The tragic news and narrative of a boy killed in the street, someone robbed in the neighborhood, or a promising future lost to gang violence has debilitated our communities.

Have we become desensitized to these narratives? How many brothers have to be killed in the street or locked in jail, for us to become enraged to create change? Just one brother killed or incarcerated, ought to charge us to say "enough is enough!" What will we do to birth a new change in our homes, cities, schools, and communities?

A lack of love that is rooted interpersonally, will ultimately leave us lifeless in our community. The statistics continue to go in one ear and out the other, with little change taking place.

While we are concerned about the plight, we must also celebrate the promise. The negative narrative of Black men, perpetuated by the media is wrong. We are determined not dangerous. We are assets not liabilities. We are scholars not thugs.

We must begin to tell the positive story, about Black men in America. Our Black men are more than negative stereotypes. We are positive prototypes, for success in our communities.

PROTOTYPES NOT STEREOTYPES

Black men are not stereotypes, we are prototypes. Due to the skewed media perceptions, you have heard enough negative statistics. The following provides analytics; according to the U.S. Bureau of Labor Statistics, U.S. Departments of Education, Health, Human Services, and

The Mystic Valley Area Branch of the NAACP:

- 1 in 3 Black males go to college.

- 3 out of 4 are drug free.

- 5 out of 9 have jobs.

- 7 out of 8 are NOT teenage fathers.

- 4 out of 5 Black fathers, living with their children, read to them.

- 82.1 percent of Black Males, (age 18 or over) have at least a High School Diploma or GED.

- 25.1 percent of Black Males (age 25 or over) have either an Associates, Bachelors, Masters, Professional, or Doctoral Degree.

- The share of Black males, ages 25 and over, who have obtained at least a Bachelor's degree has more than tripled, rising to 20.4 percent from 6.3 percent in 1976.

- Black high school graduates are three times more likely, to be in college or employed than unemployed.

- Black men make up the largest share, of people of color, serving in the U.S. Armed Forces, making up 13 percent of our nation's troops.

We have anathematized, marginalized, and stigmatized Black males far too long. It's time to start changing the narrative. There are more Black men in college, than in jail. Forty percent of Black males, are in college and/or have their degrees. Our brothers are scholars, leaders, graduates, and assets to their communities.

Don't let the media make you think that we're looting, shooting, and rioting. Black men are graduating! The picture that society has painted, primarily depicts us as incarcerated. There is a new revolution of brothers with caps, gowns, and degrees NOT cuffs, bars, and bullets! Black men are creating, sustaining, and revitalizing communities. We are changing the narrative, of what it means to be a Black man in America!

FIND A WAY, AMIDST THE WHY

People continually ask, "Why do Black/Hispanic males, join gangs and affiliate themselves with certain groups?" There are a myriad of reasons, mainly being a cohesive unit that many never received in their family. Our brothers face pressure from many angles and the "need" to conform, to a skewed perception of masculinity comes with that. The "toughest" one of us, is oftentimes in need of love the most, out of all of us. We are all looking for love, in some form or another. If you never experienced love, how can you express it?

Much too often the homes, schools, places of worship, and people sworn to protect and serve, have rejected our brothers. They are seemingly void of love. The places that have "accepted" our brothers, are the streets and the prisons. The places that should symbolize love, are often filled with devastation, malice, and hate.

There is no love in the streets, because there's often none in the home. Broken homes, lead to broken communities. You can't separate the two entities. The unspoken hardship, mental health issues, drug/alcohol abuse, physical/verbal abuse, lack of love, and fatherless homes are just some of the maladies in need of remedies.

FATHERLESS SONS

Much like many of our brothers, I too grew up in a fatherless home. My father never affirmed me. He never validated or spoke, into the essence of my identity. I am grateful for my praying mother, who raised me with love and instilled values into me. I saw her persevere, as a single parent mother, and make sacrifices for my future. I cherish, honor, and love her because of that. However, I still needed the courage, commitment, and care of my father.

Like many of us do, when a parent leaves a void in our lives, we search to fill it with things that often lead to self-destruction. I can see in the eyes of our brothers, the hurt, pain, vitriolic anger, and rage because someone dropped them and didn't nurture their humanity. Someone didn't love them. When they should have protected our brothers, they neglected our brothers.

We are living in an age of fatherless sons and daddyless daughters. As a result we are limping through life, rather than walking in our God-given power, to begin leading through life.

Yes, there are certain things, that you may never get over, but they have to be managed. Until we deal with our pain, we can never heal and create change. The pain that we carry, will translate over to the next generation, to poison our posterity. I had to find my road to redemption and forgive my father, for being absent in my life.

In much of Sigmund Freud's writings, he emphasized the role of childhood experiences, in shaping adult circumstances. Ultimately, we will carry into adulthood, what we don't heal from in our childhood. Our relationships will remain damaged, if we neglect the process of healing our mind and spirit. You can be delivered from a bad relationship, but if you haven't healed from it, then you're still in it although they aren't present.

The true healing that we experience internally, does not always happen suddenly. However, it will happen when we begin to empower ourselves, translating that into our connections and communities.

BLACK LIVES MATTER

Dr. King declared, "Our lives begin to end, the day we become silent about things that matter." No longer can we be silent, about things that matter. We don't have a license for silence. Yes, in fact Black Lives Matter.

The Black Lives Matter movement in America, has been met with much angst, by those who would seek to upend the push against police brutality. This has been a long standing problem in our communities, rooted in racism. Black Lives Matter didn't kill anybody, so let's kill the noise. Black Lives Matter, is our generation's motto of "Black Power" and "Black is Beautiful." It's our generation's, "Say It Loud - I'm Black and I'm Proud" anthem.

Those who would push against the movement vehemently scream, "All lives matter." Yes, all lives do matter. However, "all lives" are not given the same care and consideration. In a sense, White silence becomes Black betrayal. You don't have to look like me, to fight for me, just get in the fight with me.

America the time has come, to turn off the volume, on your STEREOtypes. Just because I wear a hoodie, doesn't make me a hoodlum. Just because I listen to hip-hop, doesn't make me a thug. America continues to make our

Black boys a target! They have opened jails, guns, and caskets, but closed schools, jobs, and opportunities. We are seeing that to be Black, means you're under attack. We're living in a day and age, where the ones who are hired to protect and serve, have become the greatest purveyors of violence.

Marcus Garvey declared, "The world has made being Black a crime. I intend to make it a virtue." We cannot ignore the systemic and vitriolic racism, that has been perpetuated upon our people. It has continued, from the time we were enslaved and brought to this country until now. The lives of Black people in this country, have been destroyed and undervalued for far too long.

Mass incarceration, institutional racism, voter ID laws, lack of opportunity, and inequality is cohesively connected to the fact that Black Lives DON'T Matter. Sadly 97 percent of Black males, who are victimized by

White officers, receive no justice. Thurgood Marshall, the first Black member of the Supreme Court said, "The KKK used to wear white robes, now they wear black ones."

There is a method to the meaning of the message. The reason we say, "Black Lives Matter" is to arouse the conscience of the mass majority of people, who are ignorant to the fact that we matter too. Stop murdering and killing Black people, is the cry that has yet to be answered.

Dr. Jeffrey Johnson, a noted author and consultant, has referred to the Black male, as the "new bald eagle" becoming an endangered species in society. Indeed many of our brothers, have gone from fetal to fatal. The countless fatalities, are replete throughout our communities. The hypocrisy of our democracy, will go to extensive lengths to protect a bird or bear, yet won't protect our Black bodies.

Animals get better treatment than Black people.

Regrettably, harsher penalties are given to people, who abuse and kill animals, than to those who brutalize Black people. Sadly, our African diasporic brothers, are becoming an endangered species. Black men are not seen as constituents worth protecting, but rather offenders for the purpose of incarcerating. The episodes of injustice that brought death, must be used as a catalyst to breathe life.

Rhetoric is not enough, but proactive change and policy advocacy must be the result. To escalate the message, many continue to ask the question, "Do Black lives really matter?" The answer is sometimes! In the instance that a White cop wearing blue, brutalizes or kills a Black person, is when it seems to matter.

As a people we exacerbate, the same issue when we continue to kill each other, turn a blind eye to it, and cry out against what we do to ourselves. Black lives has to matter, not just in the White House, but also in our house.

183

The animosity of Cain against Abel, slaying his brother, continues to biblically play out currently. The blood of our brothers, shed by our own brothers, continues to cry out in the streets!

Black-on-Black crime continues, to decimate communities across America. Why is it only escalated in the media, when we begin to talk about White cops that kill black people? The constant attack on the Black community, is being force-fed to make you believe, that all criminals are Black.

Why isn't White-on-White crime, given the same kind of "alarming" attention, as Black-on-Black crime? According to the U.S. Department of Justice, "84 percent of White people killed every year, are killed by other Whites." In America, Whites commit the majority of crimes. However, the portrait of those who are barbaric, gangsters, and thugs, are Black males, which is farthest from the truth.

GREEN DOLLARS MATTER

Whether it be policies, platforms, or protests many people will not agree, or believe that Black Lives Matter. In that instance, we must be prepared to show them that green dollars matter.

Our Black hands must be united enough, to economically withdraw our hard earned green dollars, from the establishment. We have a $1.2 trillion spending power. Economic withdrawal is a viable form of protest, by any means necessary!

If you don't believe economic withdrawal is feasible, then ask the players on the University of Missouri's football team. In November of 2015, the team decided to boycott, refusing to play or take part in any football-related activities, until president Tim Wolfe resigned. This came after the president refused to give any redress, to the onslaught of issues pertaining to racism on campus. As a result, the entire football team engaged in civil disobedience, by refusing to play. Seeing that the university was set to lose $1 million, if the team did not play, the president resigned.

The University of Missouri System did not make the president resign, solely because of protests, social media hashtags, or the fact that racism is wrong. It was because of the threat, of economic ramifications. If the school had to forfeit their upcoming game, it would have cost them $1 million, which sounded the alarm.

Wake up! Nothing has changed. It's just now captured with cell phones and posted to social media. The episode of this racial rage at Missouri University, was not in 1955 this was 2015! I thought we were living in a "post-racial society?" Think again. The lessons from the Montgomery Bus Boycott of 1955, teach us that economic withdrawal, is the catalyst that creates change. Black lives

may not matter to most, but green dollars matter to all.

Money talks and it screams, in the ears of the establishment!

OUR LIVES MATTER

Our lives have to matter to us. The healing in our streets,

will never come to fruition, until it flows through our lives.

Our homes, neighborhoods, and places of worship must

embody love, which has become so foreign to so many of

us. We know how to deal with hate, but so many are afraid

to love, thereby afraid of each other. When you understand,

that you are your brother's keeper, then you realize that love

is not weakness. Love is strength exercised to empower

others. Black men are not pariahs and predators. We are

protectors and providers. I am, we are, our brother's and

sister's keeper!

I AM...MY BROTHER'S KEEPER!

CHAPTER 8

Superman Syndrome

Our society is superhero driven. Media and movies are hell-bent on juxtaposing good versus evil, White opposed to Black, and villain against hero. When I was a kid, I played with action figures and idolized the "media superheroes" of society.

As a precocious boy, I wanted to leap tall buildings in a single bound. I dreamed of putting on a red cape and soaring into the skies, like Superman. As a man, I find myself seeking to do the same thing, in a different way. I strive to leap over, what seeks to limit me and soar above circumstances.

MYTHICAL MASCULINITY

Much of what is conveyed in the media, has manifested into a mythical form of masculinity. We see the portrait painted of a suave and debonair guy driving a Corvette, rippling biceps, washboard abs that you clean a shirt on, ladies that fall from the sky when you spray on cologne, and an endless supply of money that never runs dry.

The aforementioned is a silver screen shallow depiction, primarily reliant on brawn, but not brain. The mythical portrayal relies on the physical, but not the spiritual. Mythical masculinity focuses on what you have, rather than the essence of who you are. Mythical masculinity gives no credence, to being a servant leader, community innovator, father, or academic achiever. The images of masculinity in our community, have to expand beyond athletics, entertainment, and selling drugs.

Who is teaching our brothers to become real men,

189

rather than strive for mythical masculinity, with a skewed mentality? If there is no intergenerational transfer of wisdom, then we leave it to our brothers to raise themselves. Without a value system, they will play by their rules, ravage communities, and live ruthlessly rather than responsibly. Who will teach our brothers, how to be gentlemen? Who will teach our brothers, how to care for our sisters. If they are void of direction, how will our brothers protect future generation mothers and wives, who give birth to our children?

UNSUNG HEROES

Society rarely gives consideration, to the supermen who aren't rich, famous, celebrities, entertainers, or athletes. We don't applaud the unsung heroes. Whenever the topic is about Black men, the conversation generally centers on "fixing" Black men. We rarely mention the Black men who are fixing their communities. You can literally hear a pin

190

drop, when you mention the fathers who raised their children, the young men who graduated from college, or the brothers who started a business. The attitude and phraseology is, "Well, you're a man and you're supposed to do it." When you've done much with little, void of support and training, then you have in fact over achieved. You are indeed, the true gatekeepers of our communities.

THE "S" ON OUR CHEST

As brothers, we must confess, the "S" on our chest, doesn't always stand for Superman, success, or strength. Sometimes the "S" on our chest, symbolizes that we're struggling. Many times we struggle with insecurity, identity, feeling incomplete, addiction, and fatherlessness. We have been taught to repress our feelings, rather than express them. So, for years we harbor feelings of abandonment, societal trials, searching for purpose, and the reality of what it takes to be a man.

MANPOWER

When we take off our mask, uncover the machismo, muscles, and money to peer into our vulnerability, we will understand that we're more like Clark Kent than Superman. Our flashes of greatness, have been forged through the fires of grit and grief. The essence of manpower, is not in what you possess, it's in understanding your purpose. It's not in what you have, it's in who you are.

You can never know WHO you are, until you understand WHOSE you are. When you develop your relationship with God (your spiritual father), then you will exercise your purpose and power from within. True manpower unlocks the door of destiny, that you have within and serves to guide others to greatness.

MAILMAN

There is no doubt, I am a sports aficionado and a huge

basketball fan. Yes, I got game too! Don't get it twisted brother (or sister). I'm an author, but I'm athletic too.

Back in the day, during those magical Michael Jordan years, I was a big follower of the Chicago Bulls. I know I'm not supposed to say that, (being from Detroit) but it is what it is. You can't frown on six championships, during the Jordan years. However, I'll never forget the 1997 NBA Finals, between the Chicago Bulls and Utah Jazz. The story goes, that in game one of the NBA Finals, Karl "The Mailman" Malone, of the Utah Jazz, was set to shoot two free throws. To intensify the importance of those free throws, there were only nine seconds remaining in that game. If Malone, made the two free throws, it would seal the win for the Jazz.

As Malone stood at the free throw line, Scottie Pippen of the Bulls, yelled out to Malone. Pippen shouted, "Hey Karl, remember the mailman doesn't deliver on Sundays."

Scottie must have known, how to psyche out his opponent. Immediately after hearing those words, Karl "The Mailman" Malone, failed to deliver. He missed both free throws, which put the ball in the hands of Michael Jordan, who hit a shot at the buzzer to win the game. The Bulls ultimately won the NBA championship and the rest is history.

There are plenty of life lessons, that can be taken from those remaining nine seconds. A particular one, is that there will always be an opponent that seeks to disturb, distract, distort, and detour your delivery on the path to your destiny. You too are a mailman, that is packaged with purpose, power, possibility, and potential.

Don't let anybody or anything, thwart the promise of your purpose. You have to deliver, upon the promise of your destiny. The promise is not connected to money, fame, and notoriety. The promise is fashioned, by the renewing of your mind and the power of manifesting your purpose. You are a mailman. Begin to deliver empowerment in your community. Deliver in your home. Deliver on your job. Deliver and tell your testimony. If you're a believer, then you will deliver.

MALE VS. MAN

The Superman syndrome, will keep you captive to the Kryptonite of society, spinning your life in circles with no forward progress. You can have all of the outward trappings, of what a man looks like, but be void of the character that develops a man from within.

Manhood is about more than having a male body, it's the mentality which outweighs physical masculinity. Gender is what makes you male, but character is what makes you a man. It's significant to realize, that you can be a MALE and still not be a MAN. Being born male doesn't make you a man, any more than standing in a garage makes you a car.

GROWN BOYS

In this generation, we are seeing an ever increasing number of grown boys. Yes, grown boys at 30, 40, 50, and 60 years of age. Many are void of maturity and responsibility. If you only look like what you are void of, then you are a wolf in sheep's clothing. Sadly our women and children, have become victims, at the hands of grown boys who prey on their vulnerability. Real men will PRAY for you, grown boys will PREY on you.

The soulful blues singer, Muddy Waters would have referred to a "grown boy" today as a "man child." In 1955, during a time of segregation and Jim Crow, Waters released a song, *Mannish Boy*. If you listen to the song, you can hear Waters soulfully crooning and vociferously declaring himself to be a "man." He did this at a time, when black men were often referred to as "boys." Many black men were demonized and dehumanized, in an era of inequality.

196

Muddy Waters, the "Father of Chicago Blues, stepped into murky waters. As a musician, Muddy used every growl of his voice and guitar riff, as if to free himself from systemic racism and societal oppression. He sang and proclaimed "I'm a Man, M-A-N."

To juxtapose the narrative, Waters ebulliently announced his boyish ways of being "a man child and a rolling stone." Symbolically, these terms are ailments, of which we find to be in our society today. True manhood must be immersed, in a cohesion of declaration and demonstration, in our daily actions.

To only possess style and sensuality, precludes you from walking in true manhood and masculinity. Growth that only happens physically, but lacks mentally and spiritually is immaturity. Our boys will never develop into men, until we free them from a "grown boy" mentality, by teaching them to be different. To be a "full grown man" is to transition from the shadows of boyhood, into the sunlit path of manhood and brotherhood.

A real man provides for his family and protects his community. He manages his time wisely and manifests his destiny! The true test of what it means to be a man, is contained in I Corinthians 13:11, "When I was a child, I spake as a child, I understood as a child, I thought as a child: but when I became a man, I put away childish things." What are you willing to put away, in order to become? What are you willing to leave behind, in order to move ahead? What will you give up, in order to discover and gain true growth?

WHAT'S HAPPENING BROTHER?

In his acclaimed 1971 album, *What's Going On,* Marvin Gaye provided a prophetic soundtrack for society. The album is void of the sexually charged, *Let's Get It On* themes. Here we find a socially cognizant Marvin Gaye, symphonically screaming, "*What's Going On?*" He looks through his world, searching for answers, to a world riddled in shambles.

Marvin's song, *What's Happening Brother*, was dedicated to his younger brother Frankie, who returned from fighting in the Vietnam War. The world had changed and Marvin poetically commiserated, "Can't find no work, can't find no job, my friend. Money is tighter, than it's ever been. Say man, I just don't understand, what's going on across this land. What's happening brother?"

Marvin's provocatively poignant question, emanating from his 1971 concept album, lyrically reverberates today. This is not just a rhetorical question, but it seeks to engender restoration, repair, and reconciliation among ourselves and in our communities. So, what's happening brother? We continue to see calamity in our communities, constantly decimated by depravity. Our people still can't find work or adequate employment. Social security has brought about financial insecurity, for our seniors. The onslaught of inadequacy in our schools and communities, has become a breeding ground for crime. Still many, are living below the poverty line.

Marvin's question provides, the pulse and pain of the people. Gaye prolifically describes a world in a cacophony, yet harmoniously uses his voice as a symphony. His melodic voice, became a clarion call to speak truth to power. We too must use our gifts, to be critical thinkers in chaotic times.

What's going on? What's happening in our communities, brother? Our people are locked up, locked out of business, and educational opportunities. For many years, our communities have been socially engineered to become cesspools that drown dreams. We have communities, where our brothers are on the streets but not at jobs or in homes. As a result, children are abandoned and raised by mothers, without substantive support. There can be no true respectability, if you abandon your responsibility.

A grown boy/male only lives according to the constraints of his gender, irresponsibly. A real man walks in his God-given purpose, through the power of responsibility. Too many of our brothers, are suffering from an inability to accept responsibility.

MAKE ME WANNA HOLLER

Like Marvin Gaye, we're seeking to find a way and understand today. As I visit our schools and drive through our communities, it's enough to "Make me wanna holler and throw up both my hands." Marvin's melodious messages, still ring true today, as "crime is increasing" amidst "trigger happy policing." Gaye's ethereal voice continues to echo in our communities, "There's far too many mothers crying and far too many brothers dying." We must escalate love, in place of hate. We can change what's going on. You and I have the power to change, what's happening around us brother. Our communities will go up, when we step up, and help our brothers grow up!

THE MEASURE OF A MAN

The true measure of a man, is what he is willing to let go of to gain. The power of sacrifice, speaks to the measure of a man. He's not ego driven, but purpose driven. Purpose must be the engine, that propels us on the road to destiny. Mythical masculinity and machismo, is never greater than maturity.

THE MIRROR OF MASCULINITY

The impediments of our culture have produced a powder keg of emotionless, communicatively deficient, and narcissistic males in today's generation. Sadly there is a generation of misogynistic grown boys, masquerading as men, but only operating as insecure males. They exist with a false sense of bravado and mythical masculinity, which is only a shield to mask the hurt, pain, and vulnerability. The smoky mirror of masculinity, contains more shadow than substance.

Scripture warned us, "In the last days perilous times shall come. For men shall be lovers of themselves, covetous, boasters, proud, blasphemers, disobedient to parents, unthankful, unholy, without natural affection, trucebreakers, false accusers, incontinent, fierce, despisers of those that are good, traitors, heady, high-minded, and lovers of pleasures more than lovers of God" (2 Timothy 3:1-4). We are seeing this current epidemic, become a cultural pandemic, adversely affecting the lives of our brothers.

HURTS TO BE HAPPY

How can you say that you love our sisters, if you disrespect them? A true king, will treat a woman like a queen, so that she will see herself as one. Why harbor hatred against your brother? When you truly love yourself, you will express love to your brothers and sisters. We have so many brothers (and sisters), who are angry but don't even know why. They're hurting and can't even express the pain, that they're feeling. They have been so numb to pain, that it now hurts to be happy. They mask the pain with drugs, alcohol, sex, violence, and self-destructive behaviors, that never remedy the root of their issues.

Far too often, our brothers have been dropped in the home and in society. Who will pick them up? The hands that were supposed to heal and help them, only brought hurt and harm to their lives. We have not created a culture for men to be open about their hurts, flaws, and weaknesses. We have shunned and shelved it as femininity, sensitivity, and made no concession for vulnerability. If we allow our boys to be destroyed, they will never become the men that they are destined to be!

The mythical masculine culture has framed it, that when you fell off a bike as a child, you were told to "Stand up and stop crying." As a boy you were told, "Be a man." How can you be a man, in your developmental years as a child? It takes growth, maturity, and time. Our toughness must never be called into question, because we cried. It should be answered by wiping our tears and pushing ahead, despite the pain. Now, when males reach the age where they should be a man, we are seeing them choose to rebel and behave like boys.

BOND OF BROTHERHOOD

Who do we talk to, when we're dealing with issues? Honestly, there are certain things, that we can't talk to our sisters about. Sometimes we need another brother to confide in. Do we turn to our brothers and seek help, or are we too busy competing with our brothers and isolating ourselves in caves of calamity? True brotherhood goes beyond blood, it's forged by a bond. In good and bad times, a real brother empowers you through circumstances.

We must start building each other and stop competing, against each other. We know how to be smooth and debonair. We know how to act tough. We know how to put up our guard and cloak ourselves, in a false sense of bravado. We know how to act, like we have it all together. We have learned those steps, like a dance routine.

Do we know how to provide, protect, and truly empower one another? Remember, you will always fall, when you start ego tripping. Scripture presents us with a dire warning, in I Corinthians 10:12, "Wherefore let him that thinketh he standeth, take heed lest he fall." Simply, because "Pride goeth before destruction, and an haughty spirit before a fall" (Proverbs 16:18).

TRUE CHAMPION

A real man knows, that it's not how many times you're knocked down, it's how many times you get back up. Despite the odds that are stacked against you, don't give up, get up! The only way to get up, is to look up and understand that God will lift you above it. This is indeed the making of a man who, is a true champion. Make the best of your mess, A testimony out of your test, ministry out of your misery, and a stepping stone out of your stumbling block!

STAND UP

Now is the time, for men of valor to stand up and rise to the occasion. Now is the time, to rekindle the flame that was extinguished, in the vexed hearts of men. Now is the time, to take back our communities. Now is the time, to come together, because you are my brother in the bond.

An individual once said, "No man is an island." Brother, we have been working on our own far too long. If we come together, I believe things will be better. You have the power, to radically redirect and revolutionize your community. When we join forces throughout our homes, communities, school districts, and places of worship, there is nothing that can't be accomplished.

For too long, we have placed the burden on our sisters and they have carried us, as far as they can. Now the onus is on us, to pick up the pieces. It's time to direct our focus toward heaven, our family, our community, and our people to redirect our world positively.

The Apostle Paul wrote to Timothy, his brother in Christ, "I desire therefore that men pray everywhere, lifting up holy hands without anger or dispute" (I Timothy

2:8). We have lifted our hands, to hurt and harm one another, for far too long. As we lift our hands, it should be with a change of heart. Our hands must be lifted in unity, serenity, and in solidarity to become change agents in our community.

WAKE UP

Fannie Lou Hamer declared, "I am sick and tired, of being sick and tired." Aren't you sick and tired, of being sick and tired? Is there not a cause, to break the cycle of illiteracy, ignorance, and incarceration? Aren't you sick and tired, of our brothers and sisters, being slain in the streets? Is there not a cause, for which to stand and fight together? We can take back our minds, our lives, our cities, schools, homes, and communities. We can change our communities, when we change. WE CAN! The alarm is sounding all around us. Too many of us, are sleeping through a revolution. It's time to wake up!

America doesn't want our brothers, to wake up and become conscious of their power and purpose. When that happens, we become a true "menace to society." You literally become, one of the most dangerous men in America. Simply because, you have awakened the sleeping giant within you. The enemy wants to lull you to sleep with greed, drugs, criminality, lack of education, and a pseudo perception of masculinity.

When they project that 1 in 3 Black males, will spend time in prison, our righteous indignation should propel us to take action. We must declare, by any means necessary, not my son, not my grandson, not my nephew, not my cousin, and not my brother! They will not fall victim, to the manacles of oppression. We must be catalysts for change, in the lives of our brothers, from the cradle to college and throughout our communities.

Step on every negative word from critics, cynics,

haters, and naysayers. Use the negative steam, to power your dream. Step on their backbiting and use your haters, as elevators to rise to the next level. Whatever it is, rise above it. Rise above the negative and rise to the occasion.

SO YOU CALL YOURSELF A MAN?

A real man understands, that it's not about being knocked down that defines his manhood. It's what he does, after he's knocked down, that defines it. Even if you have to crawl and cry, get back up and overcome the situation.

To the world you look ordinary, but on the inside you have extraordinary power and potential. Activate your purpose, power, and potential. Brush your shoulders off. Shake yourself. Get up, man up, and get back in the fight.

You've been hit, but don't quit. Who are you, beyond what you possess? Who are you, beyond your recognition, notoriety, and success? The essence of your manhood, has nothing to do with what you have attained. It has everything to do, with who you are and what you do to inspire others.

SUPERMEN AND SUPERHEROES

We are the supermen, superheroes, and leaders that we have been looking for. As a kid, I would collect comic books. I'm reminded of those characters, who possess superpowers and supernatural abilities. You must realize, that you have untapped power and unrealized potential. It will only be discovered, when you dig into the soil of your soul. You may seem ordinary to society, but like the following superheroes, you possess extraordinary abilities:

You are an **Iron Man**, because you know how to make it through tough times and sharpen a person's mind.

You have the power of **Plastic Man,** because you are a classic man. You know how to bend, without breaking and are flexible enough to empower others.

You are **Captain America,** because you come from strong-willed people who built this country. You can rally the troops and lead by example.

You are a **Human Torch,** whose excitement and energy, can ignite someone's life to discover happiness.

You are **Mr. Fantastic,** because that's how you make people feel...fantastic!

You are **Professor X,** by any means necessary, you intellectually and communicatively empower your community.

You are a **Transformer,** because you work each day to transform someone's life on a greater level.

You are **Batman**, because you are a crusader, who stands up to injustice and defends the least of these.

You are **Spiderman,** because you recognize that with great power, comes great responsibility. You know how to use your "spidey sense" to create a web of winners.

You are **Superman,** even when the world views you as Clark Kent. You use your cape of commitment, to soar above every situation. It's a bird…it's a plane…it's a man on a mission! The "S" on your chest, symbolizes your ability, to transform struggles into strengths. You have the power to turn stumbling blocks into stepping stones. My brother, you deserve to be saluted, because you are a superman and a superhero!

REAL MEN

More than ever, there is an ardent and clarion call, for the real men in our homes and communities, to take their rightful place. It's time to man up and stand up!

Real MEN: Mentor, Empower, and Nurture. They maintain, MANage, and MANifest their destiny. They recognize their power, to overcome the odds and inspire others to do the same. Real men are true to who they are, inspiring others to be excellent through their work ethic.

Let's just be honest, let's just be real. Well, this is who real men are and this is what real men do:

Real men love God.
Real men pray.
Real men provide for their children and family.
Real men are strong husbands and fathers.
Real men lead with love.
Real men are committed.
Real men display care, character, commitment, and concern.
Real men keep their word.
Real men keep it real.
Real men uplift their community.
Real men bring unity.
Real men recognize the King within them.
Real men treat women like Queens.
Real men strengthen their sisters.
Real men empower their brothers.
Real men mentor others.
Real men show respect.
Real men provide and protect.
Real men read.
Real men are gentlemen.
Real men are genuine.
Real men have a vision.
Real men educate themselves.
Real men are intellectual.
Real men serve.
Real men turn their struggles into strengths.

Real men are hunters, warriors, and fighters
who mobilize to protect their homes and communities.
Real men are righteous.
Real men are not perfect, but they strive
to perfect their lives each day.
Real men are their brother's keeper.

I AM...MY BROTHER'S KEEPER!

CHAPTER 9

My Brother's Keeper

W hat does it mean, to be your brother's keeper and why is that significant? Seems to be a rather daunting task, to say the least. It's hard enough to be responsible for yourself, much less someone else. In a society that is inculcated, with a "me first and only" mentality, it takes transformation to think collectively and critically.

I was at a crossroads, during the prime of my teaching years, while balancing graduate education courses. I have always been enamored by the Civil Rights Movement, social justice, politics, activism, and community mobility. My mystical mentors, have always been Martin, Malcolm, and Mandela.

In 2011, I met former U.S. Congressman Hansen Clarke at a community event in Detroit. He and I served as speakers, on that particular occasion. I was empowered by his story, of how he graduated from adult education, overcame homelessness, and matriculated from the hood to the House of Representatives. We uniquely shared a connection, of overcoming obstacles. As we talked and exchanged contact information, I expressed interest in working for his staff.

CALLED TO CONGRESS

To my surprise, the next day I received a call to schedule an interview with his congressional staff. I wound up getting the position as an assistant, to accompany him during community events in the Detroit area on weekends.

Here I was teaching, going to school, and working in politics for a United States Congressman. Although there wasn't much time to rest and relax, I was excited! My plate was beyond full. I was working upwards to 80 hours per week, but I loved the hustle. I personally prefer to stay on the go. During my time as a political assistant, Congressman Clarke and I would attend, multiple events in a span of days. It was hectic. Yet as I mentioned, I enjoyed the hustle.

CHOSEN FOR CHANGE

As I became one of Congressman Clarke's primary assistants, I gleaned insight concerning community work and how to make a difference in Detroit. I enjoyed the transformative work, of "rolling up our sleeves" and working to uplift the people.

I will always have great admiration and respect, for Mr. Clarke's work. He didn't have any hidden agendas. He was a man of the people and didn't engage in "politricks."

He became a profound mentor in my life and expanded my outlook, to bring transformative change to inner city communities.

As Congressman Clarke and I developed a rapport, I informed him of my literacy/mentoring program, *Boys 2 Books*. I discussed with him in-depth, about the interconnection between illiteracy and incarceration. During one of our event filled weekends, I decided to gave him a proposal about my program. The proposal detailed ways to solve the problem of illiteracy in Detroit, our nation, and provide opportunities for boys and young men of color. He was quite intrigued and assured me, that he would peruse the proposal.

FROM VISION TO RESOLUTION

Within 24 hours, I received a call from Congressman Clarke, connecting me with his staff in Washington, D.C.

He was eager to use the proposal, to highlight the societal crisis affecting our brothers. Clarke sought to detail, the promotion of national action for literacy and opportunity, for the advancement of Black/Hispanic males. I believe he was compelled by my passion and vision, to bring change to our city. I believe all of us are chosen, to bring change in some form, this was my prime opportunity.

As I worked with his staff, we feverishly developed substantive language, which became the framework for a congressional resolution. Our work led us to develop a framework, that specifically highlighted the importance of providing opportunities, for boys and young men of color. We explicitly conveyed statistics, community inequities, and what was specifically at stake. Our resolution sought to address, what America tried to repress.

H.RES.721 IN CONGRESS

The resolution created, ultimately received bipartisan support via Congressman Tim Scott, a Republican from South Carolina. He was the first Black elected Republican Congressman, from South Carolina since 1897. This was history in the making. Even Democrats and Republicans can agree on something, every now and then.

Congressman Hansen Clarke and Tim Scott spoke at the U.S. Capitol, in Washington, D.C., to express the importance of this resolution. Each detailed their personal journey and struggle with literacy. The struggles that each has overcome and what they have become, can inspire our brothers to achieve.

On June 29th, 2012, H.Res.721 was officially introduced. The resolution expressed to the House of Representatives, that bolstering literacy among African American and Hispanic males, is an urgent national priority. This document is a public record. As a result, our

resolution in the House of Representatives, addressed the

following:

1. Recognized illiteracy as a national crisis, which
disproportionately affects African American and Hispanic
males.

2. Affirmed the goal of reducing adult illiteracy, by 50
percent in these target populations and by 25 percent
throughout the United States in the coming decade.

3. Encouraged local, state, and federal agencies as well as
the private sector, to take on literacy promotion initiatives
in an effort to resolve the crisis.

4. Encouraged federal agencies and private firms, to support
community-based organization programs and the use of
trained volunteers, to work with the target populations.

5. Encouraged the establishment of local partnerships
among service providers, to better meet the needs of adult
learners.

This was a tremendous victory, to provide

opportunities for our brothers. Many follow-up

conversations with Congressman Clarke, media, and

community organizers ensued as a result of this resolution.

After the resolution, the work continued. Congressman Clarke introduced a "Ban the Box" bill. The bill was designed to prevent employers, from asking about criminal convictions on job applications.

During one of our routine working weekends, Congressman Clarke, made a statement that I will never forget. He said to me, "I wouldn't be surprised, if President Obama uses our (H.Res. 721) resolution." He conveyed to me the congressional operations and encouraged me to be on the look out. I laughed and shrugged it off. I took his words as a simple compliment, for the great work that we accomplished. To me it was mere hyperbole. I was just a brother from Detroit, with a vision to improve my city. I never imagined, it would have national ramifications.

FRAMEWORK FOR MBK

Sure enough, in February of 2014, President Barack Obama

introduced an initiative. Our H.Res.721 framework became the impetus, for President Obama's *My Brother's Keeper* initiative. The initiative is designed to address persistent opportunity gaps, faced by boys and young men of color, to ensure that they reach their fullest potential.

One of my crowning achievements in life, is to have been at the helm of that resolution, to provide opportunities for our brothers, via the *My Brother's Keeper* initiative. There is no question, that this has become a profound moment in American history.

As President Obama introduced this initiative, he remarked, "The life chances of the average Black or brown child in this country, lags behind by almost every measure, and is worse for boys and young men. As a Black student, you are far less likely, than a White student to be able to read proficiently, by the time you are in fourth grade. By the time you reach high school, you're far more likely to have been suspended or expelled. There's a higher chance you will end up in the criminal justice system, and a far greater chance that you are the victim of a violent crime."

Our "injustice" system doesn't need reformation, it needs transformation. Not technical but adaptive, in order to uproot systemic racism and White supremacy. The penal system, has not become a place for reformation or transformation. Rather it is a lucrative plantation, disproportionately constructed to criminalize Black and Hispanic men.

MBK VISION

In September 2014, President Obama issued a challenge to cities, towns, and counties across the country to become "MBK communities." This challenge represents a call to action, for all members of our communities and mayors in particular, to ensure sustainable change through policies, programs, and partnerships.

MBK MILESTONES

According to the White House, a plan for implementation, was developed to support boys of color via six milestones:

1. Getting a healthy start and entering school ready to learn. Ensuring all children enter school cognitively, physically, socially and emotionally ready.

2. Reading at grade level by third grade. Ensuring all children read at grade level, by third grade.

3. Graduating from high school ready for college and career. Ensuring all youth graduate from high school.

4. Completing postsecondary education or training. Ensuring all youth complete post-secondary education or training

5. Successfully entering the workforce. Ensuring all youth out of school are employed.

6. Keeping kids on track and giving them second chances. Ensuring all youth remain safe from violent crime.

PREPARING OUR PEOPLE

How do we prepare our young men, to succeed in a global economy? It must begin by a succinct investment, in early childhood education and pre-literacy exposure. Family literacy and high-quality based programming, will bode well for our brothers. The inordinate amount of suspensions and expulsions must be reduced, which often leads to absences and truancy. Researchers suggest, "Black males are twice as likely, to be suspended from school, than Whites."

Mentoring and after school programs, are key indicators, to the achievement of our brothers. Role models and committed mentors are able to instill life-long values, which lead to positive outcomes in the lives of our youth. As a result, gun violence and crime is reduced.

When teachers are culturally competent and engaged in the community, there is a greater level of sensitivity to pertinent issues. Teacher and staff training/professional development must encompass cultural competency, cultivating healthy relationships, relevance, and rigor in the classroom setting. Our classrooms must not only have instruction, but they must incorporate interaction. The process of cooperative learning, should engage students and teachers to exchange ideas. The process of education, must be rooted in a shared responsibility. Teachers must have high expectations, for the students they teach and there must be mutual respect.

Tavis Smiley suggested, "Young people are like Kodak film, all they need is development and exposure." Our brothers must have exposure to career and college pathways, in order to excel. In conjunction with reading skills, our brothers need financial literacy and life skill training. Vocational and technical training, coupled with internships are needed in preparation for employment.

Contrary to some, our brothers desire to work and supply for themselves. However, you cannot gain access, to what you are not trained for and what you are denied from attaining. Oftentimes, the only door that is open to Black and Hispanic males, is a prison door. If we provide the training and opportunity to excel, our brothers will succeed and thrive in varied environments.

EMPOWERMENT AND EXPOSURE

Sadly many of our brothers, only interact with a doctor after being shot. Only talk to a lawyer, when they are defending them. Only hear from a judge, while being sentenced. Only know the police, in the manner of a drug raid, arrests, or being brutalized.

Many of our brothers want to be doctors, lawyers, judges, and yes even policemen. Oftentimes, they never meet people in these professions, until they are in a precarious position. Something is wrong, when our brothers can find a drug dealer, quicker than they can find a doctor in their community. Those of us who are in career professions, must make ourselves available to be mentors, provide internships, employment opportunities, and empower our brothers. Your presence matters!

PROSPECTS NOT SUSPECTS

Unemployment for Black males, ages 18-24, is highest in every city across this country. Access to jobs and opportunity is a necessity. Our young men have to be seen as prospects for success, not suspects for crimes.

As a further indictment, our brothers who are released from prison, face societal incarceration. They are locked out of employment and housing opportunities. A criminal record, recedes the progress of many, far after they have paid their debt to society. The ramifications of incarceration, are far reaching:

• It further distorts the perception, that people have of you.

• Disallows you from feeding and providing, for your family.

• Increases chances of being vulnerably housed or homeless.

- The system, not only incarcerates an individual, but one's family is also impacted.

- More likely to be incarcerated yet again.

As a nation, we continue to witness a greater investment in jails and incarceration, than jobs and education. The unending discrimination against ex-offenders, further incarcerates them long after they are deemed "free." Opportunities must be created for returning citizens, as they transition back into our communities.

When our brothers complete job applications and send out resumes, many of them do not receive a response because they have a "Black sounding name." Even with the same qualifications, if not more, the response is not the same without a "White sounding name." Judging a person's name and nature, to exclude them from opportunity, is yet another form of discrimination.

When it comes to being Black and Hispanic, there is a transparent ceiling on the "American Dream." Our brothers have the vision to see it, but we often lack the provision to attain it. It's not laziness. It's not lack of initiative. It's the systemic denial of access to opportunity. The power of discrimination and racism, is still rooted deeply in our democracy.

LIBERTY AND JUSTICE FOR "Y'ALL"

When will America truly "pledge allegiance" to provide liberty and justice for ALL? We're seeing it for some. We're seeing it for y'all, but we want it for ALL.

The ALL must be inclusive, of Black and Hispanic brothers and sisters. The ALL must be inclusive of those marginalized, stigmatized, and discriminated against. There must be an ALL hands on deck approach, to provide ALL access to opportunities, that have been denied. Dr. King proclaimed, "All we say to America is, be true to what you said on paper."

Impoverished communities, deprivation, drug abuse, incarceration, poor education, and a myriad of other circumstances, keep us in a cesspool of calamity. How can you thrive, when you're barely able to survive? Contrary, those opposed vehemently say, "Pull yourself up, by your own bootstraps." How can a people, pull themselves up if America took the laces and never gave us boots? Essentially, you can't expect people to use, what they have never been given. The irreparable damage of slavery, segregation, discrimination, devastation, and deprivation has crippled our communities. Is there not a cause for reparations?

Ladders for success must be created, to accelerate employment in businesses and industries, secured by African American and Hispanic males. Ultimately, it's up to us, not the President or government, to fulfill the promise of *My Brother's Keeper.* We have to do it! It's going to take us mobilizing ourselves and communities, to bring substantive change.

MBA OR NBA

Our brothers can become Fortune 500 CEOs, lawyers, scientists, doctors, astrophysicists, and assist in their communities. It takes us exposing them, to these careers and the individuals who thrive in them. We have to let our brothers know, if they never play in the NBA, they can still own the team by earning an MBA. We have to shift our brother's minds from player to owner. From employee to employer. We must build business and create opportunities.

MAKING AN INVESTMENT

We have to let our brothers know, that 92 percent of Black millionaires, did not become wealthy by shooting a ball in a basket, running on a football field, or rapping on a microphone. These individuals accrued wealth through the power of academia, by starting a business, owning property, and understanding that their network is connected to their net worth. We have to do more, than strive to be rich. We have to accrue wealth, in order to distribute it to future generations. We must make an investment, in the next generation. We have to pass the baton to our brothers, and teach them how to run the race and win!

SILVER RIGHTS

In this century, we must engage in not just Civil Rights, but develop an economic plan to ensure our Silver Rights. The power of financial literacy, will promote economic empowerment in the Black community. Why? Simply because we are the biggest consumers, and smallest investors. Much of that investment, is lacking within ourselves. We have to do more, than watch an episode of *Empire.* We have to strategically develop an infrastructure, to build an empire and economic base.

In order to do that, we must support Black businesses. As Black people, we spend $1.2 trillion annually, on cars, clothes, shoes, nails, hair weave, and other items that don't accrue wealth. Our economy has an overwhelming number of black buyers, but very few black suppliers. We do a lot of buying, but we need to do more producing and selling. We must create multiple streams of income.

Jewish people are 1 percent of the American population, but own 70 percent of the wealth. Black people are 13 percent of the population and face the greatest disparities, in economic sustainability. Before it leaves their community, the Asian dollar circulates for an entire month. The Jewish dollar circulates for 20 days. The Caucasian dollar circulates for 17 days. The dollar in the Back community, circulates only six hours and like a magic trick, "poof" it's gone!

Out of what we pour into the economy, only 2 percent of our resources, are put into the Black community to support Black businesses. Only 2 percent! If we boost that 2 percent to 10 percent, then we can create (at least) one million new jobs.

Essentially, if we as a people were to leverage our resources and combine our assets, we would be one of the richest nations in the world. If billion dollar businesses can merge, then why can't "Pookie" and "Ray-Ray" come together with a couple hundred dollars? If we divide our assets, then we can multiply our resources. Money is leaking out of our communities and we have to stop the bleeding. We will not become monetarily liquid liabilities, if we are assets to and for each other. We can't be divisive and divided, we must be united and compliant.

Financial literacy is needed, in order to bolster economic empowerment. We must make Black people, the number one employers of Black people in this century. The wealth disparity is devastating. The median household net worth of a Black family, is only $18,000. In comparison, the median wealth, of a White household is $142,000. The wealth gap in America, highlights staggering economic inequities, that plague our communities. The Black family breakdown educationally, mentally, spiritually, and economically has been systematically structured through centuries of oppression.

Corporate America is not coming to pay us. Big business and government is not coming, with "40 acres and a Mule," or reparations in hand. If it takes us economically withdrawing from larger establishments, to develop community partnerships then that is what we must do. We have to resurrect our own, "Black Bottom and Paradise Valley" and take it to the top. We have to do this ourselves. It will only work, if we work together! We must do, what

MY BROTHER'S KEEPER - DR. EDDIE M. CONNOR, JR.

every immigrant and cultural group has done and that is create our own businesses and employ our own people. Now that creates wealth! We must promote economic empowerment and substantive sustainability, in the Black community.

Every year America is "dreaming of a White Christmas." We ought to remix that, to make them dream of a black and brown Christmas. We have to support minority businesses, in a major way. If we mobilize to build a sustainable economic infrastructure, it will ensure our Silver Rights!

AM I MY BROTHER'S KEEPER?

In the words of Rev. Jeremiah Wright, "I'm unashamedly Black and unapologetically Christian." I don't care what any historian, scholar, researcher, or anthropologist has to say. I'm a living witness, that Jesus has to be a Black man. He was tried, convicted, and executed for a crime that He never committed. Now, if that ain't a Black man, then tell me, who fits the description? More than 2,000 years after Jesus, we still find Black men being executed for crimes they never committed. How can you turn a blind eye and not ask why?

There are three imperative questions, denoted in the book of Genesis. The first is presented, in the Garden of Eden, after Adam and Eve sinned against God. They sinned by eating, from the tree of the knowledge of good and evil. As a result, they hid (Genesis 3:6-12). God asked Adam, "Where are you?" It's a question that provokes one, who has lost direction. It's interesting, that God never asked Eve the question. It's a question, that God is continually asking men today. "Where are you in life? Where are you, in our communities? Where are you, in the lives of children and families?" The question should cause you to ask yourself, "Where am I?" We see the struggles that we're facing, but confused as to how we got there. Fear has caused us to go into hiding. We have hidden our gifts, power, intellectuality, ability. Much like Adam we point the blame, at everyone and everything else, except ourselves. We have gone into hiding, because we have not followed the direction of God.

The second question in Genesis 4:6, God asks Cain, "Why are you angry?" Oftentimes as men, we are angry and don't know why. Filled with rage, because we refuse to confront our issues. Bitterness, strife, and anger will hurt you long term. Unbridled anger, is one action away from danger. We must exercise self-control.

The third question, has become one of the most powerful pronouncements, since the beginning of time. The question is, "Am I *My Brother's Keeper*?" This is the first statement recorded in scripture, of a human being asking

God a question. The story of Cain and Abel, found in Genesis 4:1-12, is a familiar story. Yet it is entrenched in anger, competition drama, envy, jealousy, rage, and ultimately murder. The Bible doesn't express, how effective Adam and Eve were as parents. We don't know what family vacations, that Mr. Adam and Mrs. Eve took their beloved children on. However, we do know, within this cannon of scripture, that Cain and Abel were not reared as lazy boys. These children were born after the fall of mankind, as sin entered into the world, because of the disobedience of their parents.

Adam and Eve were sent out of the garden, to work the ground from which they were created. Adam and Eve once relished in the pristine paradise, of the Garden of Eden. Yet, were now cultivating a garden, that produced weeds, around the seeds/crops that were planted. I reckon to propose, that Cain and Abel didn't grow up with a "silver spoon" in their mouths. These boys were tending the fields, cattle, and tilling the ground. They were engaged in hard labor.

THE ADAM'S FAMILY

The first three chapters of Genesis, set the stage for human history and the fourth chapter begins to play it out. The fourth chapter introduces the first childbirth, the first formal worship, the first division of labor, the first signs of culture, and ultimately the first murder.

In my study and analysis of this chapter, I always wondered, when did Cain turn on Abel? Was his anger against his brother, built up over time? Was it episodic or was his murder of Abel pre-meditated? This particular story has the makings of a reality TV show. It's *Scandal,* and *How to Get Away with Murder* all rolled into one. This story is a "made-for-TV drama" thriller series, that would called *The Adam's Family*.

When it came time to present the offerings to God, Cain was not what you would call "a cheerful giver." His attitude towards the offering and his brother, was totally unethical. So, by the time Cain killed his brother, it was already "justified" because he destroyed him mentally, before he committed the act physically. Rather than strengthen his brother, Cain destroyed his brother. Rather than being compelled by Abel's worship, Cain competed for validation from God. This scandal has affected every corner of the world, throughout human history and continues to play out. Cain never got away with murder, because God cursed him for slaying Abel.

The denigration and degradation of men in society, rings loud and clear. The resounding question is, "Are we our brother's keeper?" This question, continues to reverberate in our communities, as we face the conundrums of our world. The voices of the abused, are crying out. The voices of slain brothers, are crying out through bloodshed.

The voices of wayward young women, are screaming for their fathers. The voices of those who are addicted and conflicted, are crying out for freedom. No longer can we turn our back, on prevalent issues in our communities. We can't live in a state of denial, with a denigrated, desecrated, and destructive spirit of Cain. We must face issues with boldness, to bring reconciliation to struggling lives.

RECONCILIATION AND RESTORATION

Now is the time, to take responsibility as men. We must reconcile ourselves to God and repair our relationships with each other. In so doing, we can rebuild and restore the lives of our brothers. If God has restored your life, then He's equipped you with power to restore your brother's life. It is critical for us to understand, that we are responsible for one another, through brotherly love.

From the very beginning, it is clear that God places a high priority, on how brothers treat each other. Cain asked, "Am I *My Brother's Keeper*?" The word used for "keeper" in Hebrew is *shamar.* This word means to guard, protect, support, and regard highly. Yet, the looming question today is "Are we responsible, for our brothers?" I believe God would respond with an emphatic reply, "Yes, we are responsible for our brothers." Not only are we our brother's keeper, but we are also held accountable for our treatment of our brothers. In our communities, we used to look out for each other, now we look away from each other. We are accountable to one another. This accountability is beyond relational, it's spiritual.

PRESENTLY ABSENT

The issue of responsibility, still hits home to me and is personalized. If you were like me, you grew up in a single parent home. My mother, did her best in trying to navigate the role of mother and "father." When in actuality, no parent can ever play both roles. I do have to give mom her props though. She taught me, how to dribble a basketball and kick a football.

Prior to my parents divorce, my father was in the house for a period of time. However, when he was there, he wasn't there. Have I lost you? When he was present physically, he was absent mentally, relationally, and spiritually.

As a young boy, I witnessed and endured the absence of my father from our household. I was perplexed, being faced with abandonment and rejection. Imagine the scars left on a child's life, who is searching for identity in society without proper rearing. You can't help, but ask the questions: What did I do wrong, for you to leave? Am I not the son you wanted? Am I not worthy of love?

So, like many fatherless young men today, I looked for a father figure on the television screen. However, athletes, actors, and celebrities couldn't fill the void. I tried to cover the hurt, through my friends and playing the game of basketball. I looked to Michael Jordan, as a "father figure" on television. I admired his perseverance, tenacity, and competitive drive. Yes, Air Jordan could soar beyond the stratosphere, yet the apex of his aerial artistry couldn't soothe my apathy, calm my fears, or wipe away the tears.

Maybe you have asked, "How can I be responsible, if I never saw it exemplified in a man?" Now, as the father is removed from the mother and the child's life, it leaves a feeling of being rejected in their lives. As a result, children begin to appropriate rejection in many forms, whether psychologically, emotionally, or spiritually.

Now, many begin to "act out" or rebel, because all they know is hurt. So, it begins to replicate in our relationships. The hurt manifests, through physical or verbal abuse, inadequacy, and lack of responsibility.

As brothers, we love to plant the seed, yet tending the soil, is where we have our hang ups. Some of the abuse at the hands of others, is replicated into sexual promiscuity, and enraptured in a psychological conundrum, because of the mistakes that our fathers have replicated in our lives.

LIFTING ME HIGHER

I can truly say, "When my father left me, then the Lord took me up" (Psalm 27:10). God is lifting you above your circumstances and previous experiences. Without a doubt, being a Black man in today's world, presents its fair share of challenges, which come with greater hurdles.

From the onset of conception, we internalize traits by which we are taught to parade our masculinity. We echo in our deep vibrato, "Yeah, I'm a man." We act, as if we came into this world as men of steel. We parade as if we're so tough, that when we were born, we didn't even cry. We often think, our power is portrayed in our physical array and display of splendor. True power is maximized, by what you possess on the inside. A false sense of masculinity, is minimized by what's on the inside. For "Greater is He that is in you, than he that is in the world" (I John 4:4).

As men, we are conditioned to refrain from expression. Oftentimes, we are so "tight-lipped" that the only thing you can get out of us, is "Yo man or what's up." What's up with that? God created us to be expressive beings.

There is no need, to repress the cognitive power or creative intelligence, that is contained within you. We often place the caution tape around ourselves, that reads, "do not cross" because of past hurt. It is to our advantage and the ultimate benefit of others, that we begin to open up ourselves. We must first open ourselves to God, to experience the magnanimity of His blessings. He has the power to lift you higher.

TRUE VALUE

Our true value, is not contained in our money or a list of women. Sexual conquests, do not quantify or qualify us. It is not a trophy or badge of honor. Romans 12:1 implores us, "Present our bodies as a living sacrifice, holy, acceptable unto God which is your reasonable service." Your body is a temple and God only inhabits, places of purity. No longer can we engage in illicit, illegal, and self-destructive behaviors, that diminish our lives. No longer can we destroy each other's lives, through violence and crime.

No longer can we berate our sisters, or call them anything

but a Queen and a child of God. Now is the time, to

improve the impoverished areas and facets of life. It

begins with improving ourselves interpersonally. We must

recognize our true value.

PASSION AND PURPOSE

God seeks to align and direct our passions as men. He

desires to use passionate men, but those passions must first

be directed towards God. As men, we are invigorated

internally with intensity and desire. The very nature of

sports, displays men who possess these characteristics. As a

result it, propels them to do exploits, in athletic arenas, even

when injured. Our passions can propel us to power, yet at the

same time, plummet us into a state of pity. Our passions are

often triggered by sensations. The world operates, from the

bases of stimulating our senses. Your passion and competitive drive, must be controlled. If not, you will make permanent decisions, in temporary situations.

BLINDED BY BEAUTY

The Motown sound of the Temptations, provided the lyrics to the song, *Beauty Is Only Skin Deep*. It was a forewarning of the temptations, that life brings. Yes, she may very well possess the measurements, 36-24-36. There's nothing wrong with admiring, it only becomes a problem when it transforms to lusting. However, albeit the grandeur of her display, you must remain alert and vigilant. Don't become so impressed by the outside, that you repress your gifts on the inside. Amidst the circumstances, you don't need a mannequin, but you need a miracle woman.

A mannequin is dressed to impress on the outside, but has nothing on the inside. On the contrary, a miracle woman has the total package, on the inside and the radiant handcrafted beauty of God, on the outside. A miracle woman is interested in you, for who you are, rather than for what you have. She's not after, what is in your pockets. Rather, she desires to help you pursue your purpose.

Never let your visual acuity, present an opportunity, that will bring disunity in the bosom of your soul. Don't allow yourself, to be blinded by beauty. It's only a skin deep mirage, that keeps you in a dry and desolate place.

God desires to take us from where we are, to where we can be. First He has to teach us individually, to help us get there collectively. If you stand on my shoulders and I propel you over the wall of life, don't just move on and leave me where I am. Since I helped you, then turn around and reach back to help me. We must reach back to mentor, inspire, and lift our brothers!

UNITED NOT DIVIDED

We must empower our brothers, to overcome barriers and rise above the wall of life. This is the vision of today, that will resurrect the lives of tomorrow. This is why Paul emphasized in I Corinthians 1:10, "that there be no divisions among you; but be perfectly united, in mind and thought."

We must uplift each other, with the power in our hands. We don't often do that, in this individualistic society of America. For capitalism is the name of the game. The motto is to capitalize on whoever, whenever, and however, for the almighty dollar. Capitalism has infused its presence, into the urban sectors of our country. The trappings of cigarettes, alcohol, drugs, and guns are at the disposal of our brothers, in efforts to wipe them out. There are more liquor stores and marijuana dispensaries in our communities, compared to all others. Society would rather have us high, drunk, and sedated than sober minded. They realize that if we ever come into the awareness, of our true power, then we will be a people to reckon with.

Capitalism resides in the casinos, that deprive individuals of their dignity and weekly dues. The name of capitalism rings loud and is audibly clear, as buildings for sexual entertainment are constructed on the corners of cities, to pervert men's minds. Capitalism has infiltrated our televisions, through materialism and greed. Our commercials solicit sexuality, through the various means of pitching laundry detergent, or selling a car.

We have been socially engineered, to focus on ourselves and not each other. We have been conditioned, to have a "dog eat dog" mentality. We are not animals, we are brothers. We can no longer continue, to pull verbal triggers that assassinate our brother's character. We must not live him lifeless, we must speak abundant life and words of encouragement into his spirit. Now is the time, for a change that will reverberate across the alleys, valleys, hills, and cities of America.

LOST AND FOUND

The Apostle Paul makes a poignant plea, in the sixth chapter of Galatians, to restore the brothers that are lost. You may be saved, sanctified, and filled with the Holy Ghost, but don't parade around with a self-righteous or sanctimonious attitude. I'm sure you can say, that you weren't always living right. Your life was immersed in sin and now you're delivered. Don't just wipe off your dirt and go about your business. Go back and help somebody else, improve their life.

Our brothers are searching, for true freedom. Your brother is struggling, to maintain his character. Another brother, is faced with the pressures of life and seeking to make sound decisions. We are all in this fight together. No one of us, is greater than all of us. We need brothers with spiritual discernment, who can probe into the hearts of the confused, misused, and abused. We need brothers, that will open their arms to the lost and assist them. If you've got yourself together, help somebody else. If you have overcome, turn around and help somebody do the same.

We may not be biologically joined, but we're joined together spiritually and in our community. In Galatians, Paul cautions us through the restoration of others, not to be haughty or high-minded. Arrogance and pride, will make you believe, that you matriculated to a higher echelon of nobility. You have to let the ego, go! We cannot be puffed up with pride. For if we begin to put our heads in the clouds, we will find ourselves caught in the same mess, that preceded our personal freedom.

Our confidence must be in something greater, than ourselves. No matter how serene or stable life seems, don't get lackadaisical and place full security in yourself. Remain vigilant and sober minded. Stop comparing yourself to other people. Oftentimes as men, that is our greatest malady. We're so competitive towards one another. Don't compare your progress to another individual. Stay in your lane and run your race, so you won't crash. II Corinthians 10:12, warns us that "when we compare ourselves, with one another, we are not wise."

TOO UNIQUE, TO COMPETE

There are more than seven billion people, on this planet. It's unbelievably remarkable, that there isn't a second you, anywhere to be found. You can search high and low, far and wide, but God only created you to do the work that He ordained for you to complete. God has commissioned and created you for a specific work to complete. Don't waste your time, trying to compete. You are totally unique.

The enormity of God's call on your life, is so expansive, that the Psalmist declared, "I am fearfully and wonderfully made" (Psalm 139:14). Nobody can duplicate, imitate, or replicate your uniqueness. You are a once, in a lifetime phenomenon. You're too unique, to compete. There will never be another you. Just do, what you were created to do.

CALLED TO SERVE

The disciples probed Jesus, to find out who was the greatest among them (Luke 9:46). We often try to validate ourselves, in comparison of where we rank against one another. It's ingrained in the sports arena, but its evident in society.

Jesus replied, "The greatest among us, is the one who serves." The least among us, is the greatest. The greatest isn't the one who is adored, idolized, or credited with a status of nobility. The true demarcation of greatness, is the power that is infused into the lives of others, through our service. Enrich the lives of others, with the gifts that God has bestowed unto you. Enrich your brother's life with the power that you have exhibited, in your time of perseverance. You are here to help, not harm. You are here to esteem and redeem, the lost at any cost. You are a restorer. You are your brother's keeper, because you are made in the image of God.

The Greeks defined the word restore as *katartizo*, which means to set broken bones back together. The word means to mend, put back together, retrieve, and reverse. In Luke 4:14-19, Jesus returned in the power of the Spirit after being tempted by the devil. He declared, "The Spirit of the Lord is upon me, because He has anointed me to preach the gospel to the poor, He has sent me to heal the brokenhearted, to preach deliverance to the captives, and recovering of sight to the blind, to set at liberty them that are bruised. To preach the acceptable year of the Lord."

Not only did Jesus claim that He is the Messiah, but He also claimed that He is a restorer. The same power of restoration that Christ has, is the same power that is in your spirit. Now it's up to you, to shake off low self-esteem, abandonment, abuse, bitterness, and negative childhood development. You have to declare, "No longer am I one of Cain's kids. I'm a King's kid, because God has restored my life."

My brother, I charge you to claim your liberty in Christ. He died and rose, so that you could live in victory. Do more than strive to be successful, but begin to live as an individual of significance in society.

CHAMPION OF CHANGE

You may be in a fight, battling opposition on all sides. You may be hurting, because your father wasn't there for you. You may be divorced, incarcerated, or suffering with addiction. You may be searching for your purpose. You may have been abused, neglected, and rejected. As you read these words, God is breaking every chain in your life. He is giving you freedom in your mind, to effectively pursue your promised future. Your past is a prison, but your future is freedom. Your past has no power, over your future. You are free to walk, in your divine destiny. You are a champion of change, called to walk in victory!

Just like Jesus called and raised Lazarus from the dead, He's calling you now. He's calling you, to rise out of dead relationships. Rise out of your cave of calamity. Rise and use your testimony, to bring unity. He desires to lift you, to a higher level of victory. You may be bound, but God is here to loose you. Yes, you might be weak, but God is making you strong. Expect to be stronger, wiser, and better because of what you have overcome.

MEN OF HONOR

Where are the men of honor? Are you a man of honor? Our world needs you, like never before. Rather than being a spectator, become an active participator in the cultivation of lives.

Our world is waiting for you to restore, resurrect, and revitalize not only your brother's life, but also the lives of women and children. You were created to be the model of God's magnitude. Take your rightful place, as a man of valor. Be the role model, that others look to for guidance. Be the man of strength and reconciliation, by dispensing the revelation of God's word in action. You may have been broken, but God is mending your soul. You may have experienced hurt, but God can heal you. The value of restoration in your brother, is not only a benefit, but a true necessity.

It's necessary that we as brothers, come together on one accord. If we are divided against each other, then we cannot stand for each other. Looking sharp on the outside, means nothing if you're dull on the inside. The world needs your sharpness, inner fortitude, and testimonies of the trials you have overcome. We must sharpen one another with ideas, encouragement, cooperation, and unity. As a result, our children and communities will sharpen and shape up. Infuse strength and vitality into the life of your brother. You are your brother's keeper!

The death of every man, diminishes who you are. Let's work to keep our brothers alive and prosperous. The blood of the slain in the streets, is crying out. Are we receptive enough to see the pain, that so many are blind to? The blindness is not simply physical, it's mental and spiritual. Empower and share your testimony, by giving insight. The young brothers may not be your biological sons, but we can't shun them. We have to adopt them.

We must extend our hands and hearts, to enrich their

lives, in order to enhance our world.

NOW IS THE TIME

In John 5:30, Jesus made a unique statement. He declared,

"I can of mine own self do nothing." The statement is quite

perplexing, because Jesus is all powerful. If anyone doesn't

need any intervention, it's Him. At least that's what we've

been taught. In dichotomy, with His humanity and divinity,

He understood the power of unity. Why do we think, we can

do everything on our own? Even Jesus understood the power

of cohesion, collaboration, and unity. The scripture

emphasizes the power of interconnectedness. Life must

engender reciprocity in relationships. We must find a healthy

balance of dependence, independence, and interdependence.

MAN IN THE MIRROR

Michael Jackson, one of the greatest entertainers of all-time, declared "If you're thinking of being my brother, it don't matter if you're Black or White." It's incumbent upon us, that we begin to look at the "Man in the Mirror," by holding ourselves accountable. When we remedy the malady within ourselves, we can then seek unity and reconciliation with our brothers.

Today is the day, to link our arms together as brothers, despite ethnicity or background. As we are linked together, let's fight the good fight of faith. Put on your war clothes, as mission minded soldiers. There is work to be done and battles to be won. There are lives in need of rescue, from the fires of futility, and the ashes of anguish. It's time to uplift and elevate your brother's confidence, stabilize your sister's life, and enhance the lives of our young people.

Work to bring transformation, in our communities and express love to one another. Your power is in your purpose, your strength is in your stability, and your restoration is in your reconciliation. You are a royal priesthood. You are a man of might and magnitude. You are a son in God's Kingdom. There is a King in you. Begin to walk, talk, act, and live like it. You are a man of responsibility, reconciliation, and restoration.

I AM…MY BROTHER'S KEEPER!

CHAPTER 10

There's a King in You

The great abolitionist, Frederick Douglass declared, "If there is no struggle, there is no progress." Indeed, where there is no progress, there is no strength. You didn't make it this far to stay where you are, move forward. Every lesson is a blessing, preparing you for life's testing.

ROYALTY

I Peter 2:9 declares, "But ye are a chosen generation, a royal priesthood, an holy nation, a peculiar people; that ye should show forth the praises of him who hath called you out of darkness, into his marvelous light." A real king recognizes his royalty and that he has a treasure within himself. In essence, he rises up to resurrect the God given gifts and talents within, by empowering himself and others.

God has not given up on you, don't give up on yourself. Be determined to turn your mess into a message, your test into a testimony, your misery into ministry, and your stumbling block into a stepping stone. I'm a living witness that God will use your setback as a setup, for your greatest comeback. He will turn your great mess, into greatness!

The strength I developed was shaped and sharpened, through adversity. Even as a teenager, battling stage four cancer, chemotherapy, radiation, and growing up without a father, I had to believe in spite of the odds stacked against me. My most challenging setback, became a platform for my greatest comeback.

SURVIVE TO THRIVE

I'm reminded, that life is not only about the drive to thrive in good times. It's also about the power to survive, in bad times. Faith gives you hope, hope gives you strength, and that strength sustains you on the road to success!

MANAGE AND MANIFEST

A real man maintains, MANages, and MANifests his destiny, by using God's MANual for life! It's time to man up and become the king that God intended, for you to be.

There is a rich reservoir of resilience on the inside, which is greater than what you possess on the outside! Never forget that the greater the obstacle, the greater the opportunity.

I CAN SEE CLEARLY NOW

Brothers, if we walk through life with the scales over our eyes, blinded by our issues, we will never see our promised future. We must become conduits of power in our communities. When you are a man with vision, God gifts you to produce, protect, and provide for the people that are in your life. Take off the scales and the mask. Walk boldly into your future, with vision as a king.

NO IS NEW OPPORTUNITY

Discover, realize, recognize, and utilize your purpose to inspire the world! No dream is unreachable, no vision is unachievable, and no goal is unattainable. You must have the faith to work for what you believe in. See every NO as "New Opportunity" and every place of rejection as direction. In the process give back, so that you can help somebody move forward!

BMW

Understand that your value is not connected, to how much money you have or what you drive. It's about what drives

MY BROTHER'S KEEPER - DR. EDDIE M. CONNOR, JR.

you. What ignites your engine and what fuels you? It's not about driving a BMW, it's about being a BMW…a "Black Man Working!"

When you realize that your identity, is infused with divinity, you can achieve your possibilities. My brother you must recognize and realize, that greatness flows through your DNA. For to whom much is given, much is required to overcome life's obstacles. The essence and power of your greatness, is ignited through the apex of your service.

BREAK OUT OF YOUR COMFORT ZONE

You may be experiencing discomfort in your life, but don't let it distract you from your destiny. At the END of your comfort zone, is the BEGINNING of your breakthrough! This is your season to deliver the vision, purpose, and promise that you have within. You're too close to quit!

You've come too far, to give up now! A true king will always win, because he won't quit.

NOT YET

On a particular occasion, I spoke at a youth event, promoting financial literacy and personal wealth. After my speech, one of the youngest attendees, approached me. As the little boy ran to me, he gave me a high five and said, "I want your shoes." I laughed, realizing that it would take him years, to grow into my size 12 shoes. I sarcastically said, "You don't want my shoes little bro, you've got the money to buy your own." He replied, "I can't buy your shoes right now, because I'm not a millionaire yet."

In the boy's precociousness and youthful glee, he didn't realize what he said was absolutely profound. His energy, comedy, and honesty, teaches us a lesson. Notice, the boy never said, he's not a millionaire. He also didn't assert, that he would never become a millionaire. However,

MY BROTHER'S KEEPER - DR. EDDIE M. CONNOR, JR.

the boy closed his sentence with the word, "yet."

The word "yet" speaks to what he believes, will be achieved, in spite of where he is right now. The word "yet" is only three letters, but it's packaged with power. Your words have power. You have to recognize and realize, that your NOT YET, is greater than your right now!

The words "not yet" can be defined, as a future existing reality that presently hasn't happened. Can you see into the future, despite your present situation? You don't need BIG faith. Just have faith, the size of a mustard seed. Maintain that faith and vision, to perceive that nothing is impossible to achieve. Where you are now, is not where you will always be. You're going higher and farther, than you have ever been.

The greatest wisdom, is not always contained in a quote from Plato, Aristotle, Dr. King, T.D. Jakes, Iyanla Vanzant, Dr. Phil, Oprah Winfrey, Joel Osteen, Steve

Harvey, or even Yours Truly. Sometimes the greatest wisdom, comes from the heart of a child!

If a little boy can say, that he hasn't achieved it YET, then why are you giving up at your age? Whatever age or stage, that you are in life, don't give up. Don't throw in the towel. Don't stop believing.

Begin to speak life to your situation, because your confession will eventually determine your possession. The term NOT YET doesn't mean it won't happen, it just conveys the fact, that it hasn't happened at this time. When a person asks, "Do you have it?" Don't say no, say "NOT YET!" It's not that you'll never be a millionaire, you're just not a millionaire YET. It's not that you won't achieve the dream, you just haven't achieved it YET. It's not that you won't get the scholarship, you just didn't get it YET. Who said you won't be married? You just haven't been married YET. Do you have the job? YOU don't have it YET! Do you have the promotion? You didn't receive it YET.

Remember the fact that your words, create your world. Your confession, will ultimately determine your possession. The power of "not yet" is the catalyst, that builds the bridge to the future, based on your confession. Begin to think positive, in every situation and see life through a new lens. Think optimistically and work to achieve the dream proactively. It may not have happened yet, but believe the vision will come to fruition!

WHAT A TIME TO BE ALIVE

You weren't born to merely exist. You were born to live with purpose, on purpose, and for a purpose because you have a dynamic purpose. When you're focused on taking care of your business, you don't have time to be in anybody else's. Your purpose for living, has to light the cauldron of your motivation each day.

Each day, you're blessed with 1,440 minutes and 86,400 seconds, in a span of 24 hours. The way you use your 24 hours, will open the door of opportunity or lock you out of it. Don't let time use you, but be proactive to use your time wisely or life will pass you by.

Since you have been blessed with life, right now is the right time to revisit the goal and forge ahead into your future. Realize that the more time, you spend looking backward, is the less time you have to move forward!

Shake yourself out of sorrow, sadness, negative thinking, and procrastination. Begin to get excited about life and life will bring the excitement, that you desire. The only person that can stop you, from living your best life, is you. Your circumstances don't define you, they refine you.

Use your time wisely, by creating your best life, through the power of your thought life. The thoughts that flow through your mind, matters most. Remind yourself, despite struggles and adversity, that every setback is a setup for victory.

Despite what it looks like, this is still an exciting time to be alive. Don't give up and throw in the towel. Yesterday is gone and tomorrow is not promised. All you have is right now! Get back in the race and remain focused. Surround yourself with goal-getters and disconnect from dream killers, by positioning yourself on the path to purpose.

OWN IT

For many people, the greatest enemy is the "inner me." When you get out of your own way, then God can create a way. Don't let anybody or anything hold you back.

There is no doubt, we have all been hurt and disappointed. Those were chapters in our lives, but it doesn't have to be the way our story ends. A few bad chapters, doesn't define the story of your life. It's not what you go through, that makes your experiences significant, it's how you handle what you go through.

GROW through the painful process and emerge with greater power! Overcome being bitter, by pressing forward to become better. There is strength, sagacity, and an undying will within you, to win at all costs. Dig deep within the recesses of your soul and push ahead, by any means necessary. You must forgive, in order to live your best life. There are certain things, that you have to let go, so you can grow.

Sometimes there is isolation and separation, right before elevation. Rid yourself of toxic relationships and negativity, that are detrimental on your journey to destiny.

Stop trying to take everybody with you, on your road to destiny. If I was driving a two-door Lamborghini Murciélago, why would I try to cram 20 people into it? It just won't work. The same concept applies to life, you can't take everybody with you. It's not personal, it's just business. Your purpose, is the preeminent form of business. Don't try to fit people from your past or present, into your future! Own the moment and make the adjustments.

Don't beg anybody to recognize your value. Some people will never SEE yours, because they're BLIND to their own! Realize and recognize, that what you have is good enough. Who you are is great enough. Where you're going, is worth working hard enough to get there! Everybody gets their time to shine and moment, to OWN IT. Don't miss your opportunity!

If you lean to your own understanding, you'll fall. Trust God through the process and you'll make greater progress. Get up, launch out, and rise to the occasion. Don't wait on anybody to create opportunities for you, create your own! No need to be needy and clingy, stand on your own two feet! Step out and take the leap. Maximize every moment and own it!

Own your greatness. Own your wisdom. Own your mistakes. Own your charisma. Own your self-worth. OWN IT and get stronger through it! Don't become bitter because of what you've been through, be better as a result of enduring what you went through! Dare to be different. Don't follow the crowd. March to the beat, of your own drum and own the moment!

STEP UP

I read a news headline with a title, "Man loses feet, but is eager for the next step." Can you overcome the odds and find faith, when doubt is clouding your mind? If you can find opportunity in opposition, power despite pain, and the ability in every disability…then victory is on the horizon!

It's interesting that the man who lost his feet, never lost a step. I know that seems ambiguous, if not contradictory. In order to "take a step" many would suggest, that you need feet to do it. However, the man who lost his feet, never lost his faith. He proves every skeptic wrong, because to STEP UP and take the leap, is greater than the activity of one's limbs physically.

However, the process to STEP UP to the next level, takes place when you transform your life, mentally and spiritually. Just because you lost something, doesn't mean you have to lose the essence of who you are. It's not about what you have, it's about who you are that makes you significant. Your significance is not in anything that you can purchase, but it's through what you will invest into yourself.

Oftentimes you gain by losing. Sometimes being the "biggest loser" isn't such a bad thing. It positions you in proximity, to becoming the biggest winner, despite the situation. The power of adversity, is the gauge that releases strength.

You have power that you haven't used yet, because the situation has not presented the opportunity, to tap into it. When your back is against the wall, when your life is out of step, and your closest advocates become adversaries, is when you must continue to press forward. You must discover a reservoir of strength, that was in you all along, but you never tapped into.

It's like living on an oil reserve and not realizing that billions of dollars, are right under your feet. It's time to use the tools that God gave you, to build, and dig deep into the substratum of your soul. True wealth is not outside of you, it's within you. It's time to become, what you were born to be.

Today is your day to STEP UP and unleash the strength, the ideas, the intelligence, and the greatness that has always been within you. We focus so much on "getting to the next level." The real question is, what are you willing to give up, in order to get there?

Within you, there is ability despite any disability. Certain experiences and situations, have tried to disable you but you must push through. When negative people try to discourage you, press through. When financial issues, bad relationships, and self-doubt, seek to stop you, forge ahead. Fight and press through everything, that is designed to debilitate your ability. The PLAN for your life, is greater than the PAIN that you've experienced in life.

Even if you have to crawl or cry, elevate yourself, and take the next step. Everything that tried to cripple you, God will use to elevate you! STEP UP and birth the business. STEP UP and enrich your community. STEP UP and challenge yourself to be better. STEP UP, step out, and stand up to transform adversity into opportunity!

KINGDOM MINDED

There's a king inside of you, to challenge the systems of society. There's a king in you, that will expand the parameters of your mind and the minds of others. There's a king in you, that will dream and not only dream, but take action. There's a king in you, that will empower communities and expose youth to opportunities. There's a king in you that has compassion for the least of these, those who are impoverished and disadvantaged.

There's a king in you, that will invent, invest, and imbibe power into the lives of others. We must dream, strive, and succeed together. We must do it so well, that the living, dead, or unborn couldn't do it any better. As Dr. King declared, "If you can't fly then run, if you can't run then walk, if you can't walk then crawl, but whatever you do you have to keep moving forward." Whatever you do keep moving forward, maximize every moment, and live through dying places. Transform every hurt into healing, think positive in negative situations, and keep your mind on your mission.

RADICAL REVOLUTIONARY

Against all odds, don't stop believing. The last four letters in *African* and the last four letters, in *American* spells "I can." Who told you, what you can't do? Who told you, that you can't be the first millionaire in your family? Who said that you won't attend and graduate from college? You can do it. You can achieve success. You can uplift the lives of others. You can think outside of the box!

These are letters to my brothers. You will beat the street. You will develop a powerful pact. You will overcome incarceration, with education and preparation. Use your gifted hands, to stir up your gift and the gift in others. Be relentless, radical, revolutionary, and resilient.

RISE AND CONQUER

Wake up the sleeping giant on the inside. Rise to the occasion and conquer! If you're looking down on your brother, it should only be to extend your hands to pick them up. When you pick them up, inspire them, and be a gateway that provides opportunity. You are more than a conqueror. Think Big. Dream Big. Achieve greater.

Rise above the opposition. Rise from your lazy bed of excuses. Rise and take back your mind. Take back your dream. Take back your education and go for it. Rise and straighten your back. Dr. King declared, "A man can't ride your back, unless it's bent." Be vigilant to have your brother's and sister's back.

KINGS AND QUEENS

My brother it's time to breakthrough. Greatness is in you. Greatness is upon you, for there's a king in you! Mount up on wings as eagles. The dream of Dr. King, lives through you. The radical roar, of Malcolm X, screams by any means necessary. The vision of Dr. Carter G. Woodson, is deep in your soul, illuminating your visual acuity. Frederick Douglas. Medgar Evers. Invent like George Washington Carver. Reinvent like Fannie Lou Hamer. Rosa Parks. Barbara Jordan. Turn pain into poetry, like Maya Angelou. Just like Dorothy Height, rise to new heights. Knockout oppression, like Muhammad Ali. Hit a home run and break barriers, like Jackie Robinson. Bring justice, like Thurgood Marshall. Pick up the baton and run, like Jesse Owens. Look at the clock and recognize it's your time, like Benjamin Banneker.

Let your ideas shine, as a light bulb, ignited by the filament of a Lewis Latimer. You're a modern day Marcus Garvey. Nelson Mandela. W.E.B. DuBois. Booker T. Washington. Stokely Carmichael. You come from kings and you surely, come from queens. Like Tupac, be the rose that grows through concrete.

Bloom where you're planted. Impact locally. Influence globally. There's a king in you, because the King of Kings gave His life for you. Live with purpose, live on purpose, and live for a purpose to inspire the world! You are your brother's keeper and this is not the time to breakdown, it's time to breakthrough. Forge ahead with your dream. There's A King In YOU!

I AM...MY BROTHER'S KEEPER!

CHAPTER 11

Every King Has a Dream

The meaning and message, of the life of Rev. Dr. Martin Luther King, Jr. is simple. Whatever obstacle that you're facing, you can overcome it. Dr. King's life embodies the fact, that the greatest leaders, are the greatest servants. We are grappling, with challenging issues in our world. This calls upon us, to reflect upon the commitment of Dr. King, to the advancement of humanity.

As you look through the lens of life, what do you see? Are you depressed or determined? Will you be faithful or fearful, hopeful or hopeless? More than ever, we must be analytical and critical thinkers. We must think critically, in the chaotic times that we live in.

DEFINE YOUR DREAM

What is your dream? Have you stopped dreaming, because of a nightmare? Have you allowed the trials of life and negative experiences, to choke your dreams? Your dreams keep you alive! Every true king has a vision and dream. The day you stop dreaming, is the day you start dying. It's time to LIVE again! It's time to DREAM again! It's not too late to be great and it's not too early to get started.

The freedom fighter and fiery orator, Dr. King proclaimed truth with determination and ebullience. He spoke of "the fierce urgency of now." He implored us, to rise above difficulties and manifest the dream of equality for all.

There are a myriad of issues, pervading our world today: education, the economy, health care, poverty, gun control, mass incarceration, violence, and the list goes on.

Yet education remains preeminent, because as our education system goes, so goes our nation. Lack of education, limits access to opportunity.

CREATED EQUAL, TREATED UNEQUAL

America is a mixed bag of religious beliefs. Many idealists pledge allegiance, to America's standing as a Christian nation, when in fact that may not be true. According to the Pew Research Center, the U.S. public is becoming less religious. "The religiously unaffiliated, now account for 23 percent of the adult population." We're finding more people, opting to sit on their sofa and watch sports on Sunday, than assemble in a sanctuary.

In fact we are racially segmented and separated, at no greater time than on Sunday mornings. In fact, Dr. King affirmed, "11 a.m. on a Sunday morning, is the most segregated hour in this nation." The lack of diversity in many American churches, is often rooted in racial

segregation, than religious style of worship. We find that

the advent of secular humanism is on the rise. There is a

growing number of people, choosing to reject religious

dogma, to opt for a non-religious lifestyle.

Many staunchly argue that America was built on

Christian principles, because of the phrase "in God we

trust" which is embossed, on U.S. currency. The framers of

the U.S. Constitution and Declaration of Independence,

were not Christians but Deists. They believed that human

reason was a reliable means, of solving social and political

issues. The philosophical beliefs of Deism, are

fundamentally rooted in the belief, that a supreme being

created the world and then removed himself from it.

Essentially there is no reliance, on religion or celestial

authority.

The Declaration of Independence (1776) affirmed,

"We hold these truths to be self-evident, that all men are created equal." In actuality, the document relegated that power, to rich land owning White men. Thereby, you can read between the lines, that "all (wealthy White) men are created equal." This in fact, highlights the "truths" that are "self-evident." Ironically the document was written, by wealthy White men, who were also slave owners.

The aspect of being "created equal" and treated equal, are totally separate things. Black people have yet to receive equal treatment. Our living conditions, the schools, the communities, and oftentimes even the law is perpetually unequal. Time and time again, the law has not protected us. In fact, it has been manipulated to prosecute and neglect those, who should receive justice. The covert and overt forms of oppression, continue to stifle the progression of African Americans.

HARVEST AND HABITS

The question that we must ask ourselves, is "What can I do, to make the world a better place?" Not just presently, but for future generations. There is a great work for all of us, to engage in. We must labor, in order to reap a plentiful reward. There are no shortcuts in life. If you take shortcuts, you will get cut short. We must understand, that there is power in our productivity!

The Greek philosopher Aristotle declared, "We are, what we repeatedly do." What are you doing, on a daily basis, to repeatedly be successful? What positive habits, are you forming? Your harvest is connected, to your habits. Who are you surrounded by, in your personal circle? Your relationships and friendships, have a direct impact on your future. I can tell the outcome of your future, based on your present friendships. What words are you saying? Are you speaking negativity, to yourself and others? You will create or destroy your future, through the power of your words. Speak life and begin to empower yourself and others.

PORTRAIT OF POWER

Historians have detailed, that in Dr. King's early life, he would read books incessantly. While growing up in Atlanta, Georgia he literally drove adults crazy, because of his curiosity that evoked questions. Even as a young boy, he worried about people who didn't have enough to eat. As a precocious and intelligent child, he graduated high school, at the age of 15. Even at a young age, Martin had a strong sense of destiny. After earning his Ph.D. in systematic theology, he served as the Pastor of Dexter Avenue Baptist Church.

He became a prominent leader, in the religious and civic community. Dr. King advocated a social gospel that connected, Jesus with justice. It's rather evident, that the life of Dr. King was accelerated beyond his peers and young years. Little did he know, that he would only live to be 39 years of age. Yet in that brief time, he changed a generation.

TIME IS OF THE ESSENCE

None of us know, how much time we have. It's imperative that we live each day, to maximize our purpose. Just like Dr. King, you are on a crash course with destiny. It's time to unearth and dig up the greatness, that is within you. You are special, significant, gifted, and valuable. You are life's "red box and gold bow." You are a gift, to the world. Each one of us is gifted, but the tragedy is that some people never open their package.

The best of you and me, resides in the power of our psychology, mentality, spirituality, and the enormity of our destiny. We must expand the parameters of our mind and think BIG. Your vision, idea, and dream must be bigger than your environment. Supersize your dream!

Why try to fit in, when you were born to stand out? Embrace your uniqueness. You're too extraordinary, to be ordinary. Manifest your destiny. It's your time! Pursue your purpose, overcome obstacles, and become a preeminent voice for your generation.

LEARN, EARN, RETURN

We must be quicker to learn and listen, than to teach and train. We must have a receptive ear, to hear from one another. Thereby, we can grow and overcome adversity together. Dr. George Fraser said, "Once you learn and earn, then you must return back to your community." We must give back, to empower others to move forward. The resources that you have received, through education and experience, must be used as a tool to build lives. You have a mandate, to go back where came from and help somebody. Who is more equipped to go back and help, than those who endured trials and triumphed?

BRIDGES OF BREAKTHROUGH

We must bridge our differences and embrace the power of our diversity. We must see strength in diversity, rather than weakness and adversity in diversity. Our diversity should unite us, not divide us. Our communities, are at a precarious intersection. It's either education or incarceration. Maybe not physically, but it can be a psychological imprisonment.

Chains are not only metal, but they are also mental. The chains of psychological and economic depravity, are designed to cripple our progress and mobility. We must empower our youth, to recognize their potential and activate their purpose.

DIGITAL DIVIDE

We have become so inundated with technology, being

interwoven in our wired and wireless world. Although we are connected, we are disconnected more than ever before. The advent of social media, has engendered a generation of many who are socially inept. They can text, but won't talk. They know code, but can't formulate a conversation. This is an "LOL, TTYL, GR8" generation. If you don't know any of that text lingo, I suggest you search on Google "L8R." To the disdain of many teachers, our children continue to write, like they text on their phones.

In a world that promotes narcissism, we have adopted an "all about me" mentality. Even the names of technology devices, reflect that mindset. We live in a world, of Facebook, Instagram, Twitter, and YouTube pages. We have iPods, iPads, and iPhones. It's an "I and me" not "us and we" culture. Rapper Lil Wayne, rhetorically exclaimed, "I'm all about 'I' give the rest of the vowels back."

Dr. King never had an email address, cell phone,

social media page, or access to many of our technological amenities. However, he and many others, mobilized a movement through the power of unity. If they did much with little, how much more can we do, with what we have? What resources will you use, to uplift the masses?

Don't tell me, that you don't have the power to empower yourself. You have power in your mind and hands. How will you use it? You are your greatest resource. Discover the king in you. Unlock, stir up, and release the gifts that are within you. For to whom much is given, much is required. You have been given much and much more is required of you, to enhance our world.

AMER-I-CAN

Whether Black, White, Asian, Hispanic or any other ethnicity, regardless of background, we are American. Not all of us came here willingly, but we are all here collectively. The last four letters, in *American* is "I can." Encourage yourself and say, "I can be successful. I can achieve my goals. I can move forward. I can forgive. I can live. I can uplift the lives of others." When you believe that you can, by engaging your mind and will…then it will happen!

Begin to think outside of the box. When you're dead, they will put you in a box. So while you're alive, you might as well think outside of the box. This is the year and right now is the right time, to expand the parameters of your mind. Push past limited thinking to unleash your unlimited dreams. Approach every obstacle, with dogmatic determination. This will serve as a stimulus, to reach the apex of opportunity.

It's argued that no one did that more, in the last century than Dr. King. He was one who believed in freedom, justice and equality for all. He desired to establish "The beloved community" where love and peace, would become the governing norms and guiding principles of society.

STRENGTH TO LOVE

Regardless of race, Dr. King stood for the liberation, of the oppressed. He practiced non-violence and expressed love, in the face hate. The portrait of Dr. King, has often been politicized. He was not a one-dimensional, utopian dreamer void of an action plan. Rather he believed, in the relevance and reality of equality. He was one who challenged, the inequities of America. He challenged the establishment and awakened the conscience of society.

Dr. King served as a trumpet, of moral conscience in America. His melodic voice, provided a prophetic clarion call to stimulate action. He emphatically declared, "Cowardice asks the question, is it safe? Expediency asks the question, is it politic? Vanity asks the question, is it popular? But conscience asks the question, is it right?"

He challenged our nation and the world in a greater context, that "We must learn to live together as brothers, or perish together as fools." Dr. King proclaimed, "The ultimate measure of a man is not where he stands, in moments of comfort and convenience, but where he stands at times of challenge and controversy."

CONSCIENCE OF A KING

We must understand that Dr. King, fought for the oppressed, underserved, overlooked, and underrepresented. He was for the poor Whites, Blacks, Hispanics, and Asians. America loves to freeze the image of Dr. King, to August 28, 1963. As he proclaimed his "I Have A Dream" speech, to more than 200,000 people at the March on Washington.

King's life was more than an episodic "Kumbaya moment." Yes, Dr. King spoke about the dream, but he also mentioned the nightmare. He said, "We can never be satisfied, as long as the Negro is the victim of police brutality."

Dr. King spoke truth to power. He was not docile. He was defiant and engaged in civil disobedience. Dr. King was courageous enough to speak out, against the Vietnam War, on April 4, 1967.

THE TRIPLE EVILS

Dr. King talked about the triple evils of society: poverty, racism, and militarism. He spoke candidly about racism and launched a war on poverty via *The Poor People's Campaign*. Dr. King spoke against the inequities, of people in impoverished communities.

America is the richest nation in the world, yet people go to sleep hungry every night. America boasts of being the land, of "milk and honey" but people sleep on park benches. How can we purport to be the richest nation in the world, and not take care of our own people? Dr. King affirmed, "Poverty is the bride of crime." Wherever you see poverty in a community, crime is sure to follow. Essentially, if we are to eliminate crime, then we must address poverty.

Dr. King never attacked people personally, he addressed the policies and issues. He went to the root of the problem and the heart of the matter, to bring transformative change. He was a man with flaws like all of us, yet he remained faithful to his purpose. Just as Dr. Martin Luther King, Jr. empowered others, standing for equality and ethics, so can YOU!

As we and future generations, remember Dr. King and his dream, I encourage you to press on and keep pressing. In spite of looming pessimism, he was optimistic, to express "Even if I knew that tomorrow the world would go to pieces, I would still plant my apple tree."

We must plant seeds of strength and sagacity, to reap a harvest of hope. We must come together, as true keepers through the bond of brotherhood. Dr. King declared his dream, "that the sons of former slaves and the sons of former slave owners, will be able to sit down together at the table of brotherhood." We must come together at the table of brotherhood, to bring love and light into our homes, churches, schools, and communities.

Brotherhood extends beyond blood relation or skin complexion. It's a true bond of connection, that incorporates reconciliation, respect, and reciprocity to uplift one another.

You are a king with a dream. Develop action steps, to ignite your dream and bring your vision to fruition. Every king must work to build their dream, to provide for communities and future generations. This is your time to bless the world with your gifts and talents. When God is your Source, you will have the resources!

A prayer of breakthrough, for my brother:

Father, empower my brother to be a committed, compassionate, and caring man of standard. Strengthen him to overcome every obstacles. Expand his thinking to create opportunities and turn ideas, into income. Break every generational curse over his life. Grant my brother favor and power, to walk in victory as a king in his home, church, community, school and place of business in the name of Jesus! You are free, to walk in victory!

I AM...MY BROTHER'S KEEPER!

Reclaiming a Nation

How can we reclaim a nation, that is bound
by the manacles of capitalism,
perversion, frustration, and degradation?
In the words of Langston Hughes,
"Let America be America again,"
but I propose to you, where does America begin?
From the ghettos and gangs,
to our brothers locked behind bars,
physical and psychological chains.
From teenage pregnancies, to economic inequities.
From drive-bys and chalked out crime scenes,
to sexually explicit music videos and
violence on TV screens.
Makes you mad enough to holler, yell, and scream.
Have we become more technologically minded,
yet day after day, morally blinded?
How can we reclaim a nation?
Our hopes and dreams
reside in the hearts of young people,
who are often confused,
because they've been misused and abused.
Fathers have fallen and mothers are crawling,
to pick up the pieces, that have been left behind.
Politicians are speaking and
Preachers are preaching
but who is reaching, out to the lost,
so that they can be rescued at any cost?
Where are the leaders,
that seek to uplift our society?
What are the servants, in our community?
Who will work to bring unity?
Where is the strength that will,

"Hew out of the mountain of despair, a stone of hope?"
Who will step up and be, their brother's keeper?
Their sister's protector?
Where is the love, that will embrace the hater?
Where can America turn,
when it has turned on herself and her creator?
In order for America to be,
it must begin inside of you and me.
In order for America to be,
Christ must live in our hearts
where He can invigorate spiritual liberty.
So, to all who read this decree
Let not your heart be troubled.
For the answer to the reclamation of a nation is
found at the cross of reconciliation.
With this faith, we can wipe away the tears of
frustration and degradation.
So, for this to become true, it must begin inside of you.
Not just in the White House, but your house.
Not just on the east and westside, but every side.
For the band of brotherhood and
the serenity of sisterhood,
must begin in your neighborhood.
For we must break down the barriers,
that blockade our benevolence.
To reclaim our nation,
we must be determined, dedicated,
and devoted to uplifting humanity.
For this cannot be all of me and none of thee.
Our nation's declaration was built upon
freedom, liberty, and equality.
So, let us live together as brothers,
rather than perish as fools in hypocrisy.

SIX BUILDING BLOCKS - BOYS/MEN

As a bonus, here are *six building blocks, that every boy needs, to become a strong man:*

1. Book

Every brother, needs a book to invest in himself and deposit knowledge into his mind. The average American reads one book per year. The average CEO, reads at least 30 books per year. Increase your vocabulary and wisdom. If you want to lead, you've got to read! The greatest book that transformed my life, is the Bible…a true MANual for living abundantly and becoming a Godly man!

2. Bank account

We are a consumer based society. We are programmed to purchase, rather than create and invest. Develop an understanding of currency and the value of money. You need more, than a Louis Vuitton wallet and a checking account. You need a savings account. Saving your money, puts you ahead of the game. Investing it in your dreams, helps you to win the game. Don't chase money, chase purpose. If you chase purpose and work your gifts, money will chase you. Understand the laws of money and you will increase your value.

3. Watch

Every man needs a wrist watch. It doesn't have to be Gucci, Fossil, or Movado. For all that matters, it can be a Quartz watch. It's important to always know what time it is and the season we're living in. This is beyond just chronological, this is cultural and spiritual.

As you are aware of time, be sure to value your time. Your time is greater than money. If you lose money, you can get it back. When you lose time, it's lost forever. Psalm 90:12 declares, "Teach us to number our days, that we may apply our hearts unto wisdom." Your time is precious and priceless. Don't waste your time and don't let anybody waste it!

4. Belt

We criticize and demonize our brothers, for their sagging pants. To many, it has become an "eyesore" in our schools and communities. We criticize sagging pants, but not sagging homes, sagging schools, and sagging communities. I'm not excusing or condoning it. I'm just addressing it. We have to "pull up" and remedy the issues, that are an impediment to the success of our brothers.

We must develop connections with them, in order to empower them. As a result, they will "pull up" their sagging goals, sagging dreams, sagging grades, and yes even those sagging pants. We tell them how not to dress, but will we show them how to dress?

5. Tie

I'm grateful for my Grandfather, Harry Smith, Jr. He was a teacher, coach, mentor, deacon, war veteran, community advocate, and a family man who loved God. He became a surrogate father in my life and I celebrate his life and legacy. He was always dressed like a gentleman. I remember being a little boy when he taught me, how to wear a neck tie. As he taught me how to wear it, he gave me a valuable lesson.

He said "Edward, if you're good at what you do, you'll never have to tell anybody. They will tell you." In turn, I serve as a mentor to our young brothers. It's my way of paying the legacy of my grandfather forward, by teaching them how to wear a tie in the same fashion. I always tell my brothers, "Dress for success, dress to impress, and dress the way that you want to be address… because you're TIED to success!"

6. Mentor

So many of our brothers, are void of mentors. You can't lay claim to success, without having a successor. Your greatness lives on, when you pass the baton to someone else. You must share your knowledge, wealth, and wisdom with a generation of brothers. They may not look like you, dress like you, listen to the music that you enjoy, or have your experiences. However, our brothers need your time and commitment.

We can't expect our brothers to be a man, if they don't see and interact with one. Boys will be boys, until a man teaches them to be a man. A real man will manage, maintain, and manifest his destiny through the lens of responsibility. As a result, he will mentor and teach another brother to do the same. Our brothers need real men in their lives to mentor, motivate, and empower them to manifest their destiny daily! We have what it takes, let's step up to the plate!

Terry Tempest Williams declared, "The eyes of the future are looking back at us and they are praying for us, to see beyond our own time." Our young brothers are the future. We must have a vision for their future and work to build their lives, for the future!

I AM...MY BROTHER'S KEEPER!

ACKNOWLEDGMENTS

As I think in retrospect of my life's journey, it has prepared me for this opportunity to empower you. I am appreciative of the struggles and strengths, which equipped me with wisdom to share my knowledge and experience.

Truly with God all things are possible and without Him none of this would be possible. He is the ultimate strength and sustainer of my life.

I must acknowledge my dear Mother, Dr. Janice K. Connor. She is an educator and minister of 30 years, whose love has propelled me forward. I love and appreciate you!

To the most dynamic professors, that I've been blessed to learn from: Dr. Esther Coleman, Dr. Vivian Johnson, Dr. Jonella Mongo, and Dr. Christina Murriel.

Hansen Clarke, I will always be appreciative of the experience, to work as your assistant in Congress. Continue to be a trailblazer of ingenuity, in our community.

Trabian Shorters and my BMe brothers, across the country. Your guidance and brotherhood, has made me a stronger man today. You inspire me to REACH higher!

I am a product of the privileges, that Civil Rights has afforded me. I stand on the shoulders of giants, our sainted ancestors, Civil Rights icons, and nameless leaders, who never gave up. Your vision for Black men like me, has caused me to empower Black men that will come after me.

To all of my young brothers, past and present, in the *Boys 2 Books* program. The greatest honor has been to witness your growth and graduation. I've learned life lessons, through the obstacles that you have overcome. Brothers, I salute your tenacity and toughness, to never give up. Success is in your mind and in your hands. Keep leading and succeeding!

ABOUT THE AUTHOR

DR. EDDIE M. CONNOR, JR. is a resident of Detroit, Michigan and grew up in Kingston, Jamaica. He is an Author, College Professor, International Speaker, Minister, and Founder of the *Boys 2 Books* literacy/mentoring program. Dr. Connor empowers people to overcome obstacles and walk in their unique purpose, by sharing his story of overcoming stage four cancer. He has earned a Doctorate and serves as Graduate Education Professor, at the prestigious Marygrove College.

While working alongside, former Congressman Hansen Clarke, Dr. Connor's efforts assisted in developing a Resolution in the 112th U.S. Congress (H.Res.721), to express that bolstering literacy amongst African American and Hispanic males, is an urgent national priority. The development of the resolution, became the impetus for President Barack Obama's, *My Brother's Keeper* initiative.

Dr. Connor has garnered prestigious honors, for his community activism and unique leadership ability, such as the Dr. Martin Luther King, Jr. Humanitarian Award, NAACP Speaker Award, Black Male Engagement Leadership Award, The Spirit of Detroit Award, and named one of the top 100 leaders in *Who's Who in Black Detroit*.

Dr. Connor has been featured via BET, CBS, FOX News, NBC, PBS, TCT, The Steve Harvey TV Show, The Tom Joyner Show, The Word Network, USA Today, and many other media outlets. He was also featured in the acclaimed BET documentary, *It Takes A Village to Raise Detroit*.

Dr. Connor speaks extensively on the subjects of education, leadership, overcoming obstacles, and maximizing your purpose. As an international speaker, much of his work extends throughout Jamaica and South Africa. Dr. Connor empowers people at churches, conferences, community centers, and colleges, by inspiring and motivating others to overcome the odds.

TELL YOUR STORY

Share your story, with Dr. Connor and *My Brother's Keeper*. Do you know a strong brother, in your school, university, place of worship, or community? If you or someone you know, has overcome adversity, succeeds academically, or advocates for their community, please share the story. Email or write to:

info@EddieConnor.com

My Brother's Keeper
29488 Woodward Ave. Suite 215
Royal Oak, MI 48073

WEBSITE:
To learn more about *Boys 2 Books,* visit:
www.EddieConnor.com

SPEAKING ENGAGEMENTS/ MEDIA REQUESTS:
info@EddieConnor.com

SOCIAL MEDIA:
(Facebook, Instagram, Twitter)
@EddieConnorJr
#MyBrothersKeeper
#MBK

68120562R00203

Made in the USA
Lexington, KY
03 October 2017